THE REALLY INTERESTING QUESTION
and other papers

THE REALLY INTERESTING QUESTION

and other papers

LYTTON STRACHEY

Edited and with an Introduction and Commentaries by
PAUL LEVY

COWARD, McCANN & GEOGHEGAN, INC.
NEW YORK

CONTENTS

EDITOR'S NOTE

When Lytton Strachey died in 1932 he left thousands of pages of unpublished letters, essays, stories, plays and poems to his brother and literary executor, James Strachey. On James Strachey's death in 1967 these passed, along with his own papers and a great many Strachey family papers, to Mrs Alix Strachey. Mrs Strachey, wishing to see this enormous archive maintained properly, has made a gift of these papers to the Strachey Trust, a registered charity, whose tasks include not only looking after this and similar bequests, but also establishing the modest nucleus of a central catalogue of papers of this sort.

This is the second volume of hitherto unpublished Strachey papers to be issued, and with the mammoth exception of his correspondence – to appear several years hence – the most important of Lytton Strachey's literary remains are now in print.

The editor wishes to thank Mrs Alix Strachey, who blessed this undertaking and read parts of the Introduction and the Afterword in manuscript, and Michael Holroyd for his generous encouragement.

INTRODUCTION

The works Lytton Strachey published in his lifetime are the products of a careful and exacting craftsman; they are finished objects, highly polished, with a brilliant surface that shows no trace of the joins. It is a great tribute to his art that forty years after his death his books are still read for pleasure; one would be unlikely to turn to *Eminent Victorians* for instruction, for the four biographical sketches it contains are too short to convey much information to the serious student. *Queen Victoria* and *Elizabeth and Essex*, too, continue to appear, often in new editions, though they have been superseded, as biographies, by newer and fuller studies. It is hoped that the present collection of hitherto unpublished Strachey writings will also give pleasure to the reader, some of them for their literary merit, and others for quite different reasons. Some of the pieces were not published during the author's lifetime because they were experimental, some because they were ambitious failures, and some because they were unfinished. But most of them were not intended for publication at all.

Few authors writing today will leave behind them a substantial body of private or esoteric work: they work as professionals, with a view to eventual publication, or as journalists, for immediate publication. In the more leisurely age when Lytton Strachey lived and wrote, it was not uncommon, even for such a conscientious writer as he was, to produce occasional pieces for a very small audience of friends, with no idea at all of publication. The body of work that Strachey prepared for publication is not large: in addition to the works mentioned above, *Landmarks in French Literature* and a few volumes of essays and reviews complete the corpus and in fact the esoteric work totals nearly as many words. There are essays written to be read aloud to the Cambridge Apostles and other University societies, or to groups of friends in London: there are plays, some of which were acted before private audiences; there are stories, like the recently published *Ermyntrude and Esmeralda*, that passed from friend to friend and were occasionally read by Strachey himself as part of an evening's entertainment on a country week-end; there were experiments in literary form, such as dialogues, and an attempt at a political novel. And of course there was the verse, some of it rude, much of it erotic, but all of it romantic, written to delight Strachey's Bloomsbury friends, who sometimes refer to it in their letters. Correspondence, too, may be considered part of Strachey's private work; and even from the few letters that have been published – to Virginia Woolf and to Carrington – it can be seen that, though not writing for publication, he exercised a great deal of care in his correspondence.

Nearly all the private or esoteric works show a rather different aspect of his mind than do the published ones, and undoubtedly have an important contribution to make to an understanding of his character, of the style of life of his close friends, and of the circle in which he moved. The present collection has been chosen to cast a slightly different, perhaps less harsh, light on them than usual. Bloomsbury has often been accused collectively of insularity, of lacking a social conscience, and of being overly self-regarding; it has even been said that Maynard Keynes was looked at askance by his Bloomsbury friends for his work at the Treasury and for his involvement in the world of political affairs. This collection, while not unrepresentative of Strachey's unpublished writings, is designed to temper such an impression, and many of them have been chosen for their bearing on social questions as well as for their entertainment value.

The pieces are arranged thematically in three broad and not very strict categories. The first, "War and Politics", concentrates upon questions of peace and war and includes a selection of Strachey's correspondence with his brother James for the year 1916; their letters are chiefly concerned with the issue of conscription. There is also a dialogue on the theme of war, a selection from an unfinished novel which was to deal with topical political issues and events, and an essay delivered to the Cambridge Apostles which explores some very general questions of morality and action. The second section, "Men, Women, Sex and Art", is composed of pieces on morality in art and literature, on censorship, on the role of women in society, and essays and dialogues on relations between the sexes, on marriage, on population- and birth-control, and on sexual morality and practices. The third group, "Pieces from the Margin of Literature", contains four short stories with homosexual themes and a poem about an experience with drugs.*

Strachey went up to Trinity College, Cambridge, in 1900, and the

* This last is the only piece in the collection that has been published previously (see note to poem, p. 166). Portions of the 1916 correspondence have been quoted in Michael Holroyd, *Lytton Strachey* Vol II, 1968.

earliest pieces here date from his undergraduate period. One evening in 1902 he and J. T. Sheppard of King's were each visited in their rooms in college by a more senior undergraduate who informed them that they had been elected members of the Cambridge Conversazione Society, that distinguished and most famous of all discussion clubs usually known as the Apostles, which had been founded by George Tomlinson in 1820. Although opaque references to it had appeared in Tennyson's *In Memoriam*, and quite transparent ones in the biographies of several eminent members, the Apostles was still a secret society; wives apart, membership might not be disclosed until after death. Had its existence been generally known among undergraduates, there would certainly have been competition to join this most remarkable body of dons and undergraduates; and so it was in an atmosphere of stealth that their election was made known to Strachey and Sheppard (who later became Provost of King's).

Rather a lot of ritual was associated with Apostles' meetings. The gatherings took place on a Saturday night, when the "brother" to whom the lot had fallen the previous week would read aloud a paper on an assigned topic. He would read standing on the hearthrug, and afterwards lots were drawn to determine the order in which the brothers would speak. It was obligatory for each member to take his place on the hearthrug when his turn came to speak. Following this ritual, the question would be put; the proposition to be voted on need not be the one proposed by the evening's reader, but it generally grew out of his paper or the discussion of it. Whales (sardines) on toast and coffee were consumed, the topic for the next meeting was decided, and lots were drawn to determine the reader. A tame enough affair, it might appear. But when Strachey was reading the papers reproduced here, the intellectual level of his audience would have been formidable. First there was the great philosopher G. E. Moore, at this time the most influential of the Apostles. Goldsworthy Lowes Dickinson, a don at King's and also a philosopher, might be present; "Goldie's" mind might not be so precise as Moore's, but he had a knack for detecting insincerity in argument. While it was normal, even usual, for the papers read to the Apostles to have a rather flippant tone, a high degree of real conviction was mandatory. Bertrand Russell might well have dropped in to hear one of Strachey's papers; and Desmond MacCarthy, who was to become England's leading literary critic, often came up from London to hear one of the new brothers read on a Saturday evening, as did Robert Trevelyan, the poet, and Charles Sanger, the famous barrister. In the early days, Strachey's audience might have included the brilliant Llewelyn-Davies brothers, E. M. Forster, G. M. Trevelyan and H. O. Meredith, the economist.

Among Strachey's contemporary Apostles were Leonard Woolf,

John Maynard Keynes, and Saxon Sydney Turner, who, like Moore, was fanatical about music. Strachey returned to Cambridge to read papers several times in 1911 and 1912, and his audience would then have included his brother James, who was to become an eminent psycho-analyist and the translator of Freud, as well as Rupert Brooke, Gerald Shove, the economist, and Harry Norton, the mathematician. Another new brother in 1912 was Ludwig Wittgenstein, who was soon to make a revolution in philosophy; indeed, almost all the main developments of twentieth-century philosophy in the English language were to grow out of the work of Apostles, and the Apostolic contribution to economics was to include not only that of Keynes, but also those of Ralph Hawtrey and the short-lived genius, Frank Ramsey. Several eminent scientists were members, as was the great mathematician G. H. Hardy.

At the time when Strachey became an Apostle, in 1902, it was Moore who set the tone of the discussions, and his example could be seen even in the style of the papers read to the Society. But to later generations of Apostles, Strachey's influence was also evident. Moore's contributions to the Society, while not devoid of humour, were always deep and searching; when Moore endorsed a view he always believed it, and would defend it with passionate sincerity. Strachey, though never insincere, added to the Apostolic style a certain note of levity. He taught the brothers that it was possible to deliver one's most deeply felt convictions in a sophisticated and often funny tone, a tone that, while not apologetic or self-deprecating, showed an awareness of the relative worth of one's opinions and arguments. Strachey perfected the paradox of tone: he spread a layer of wit over the Mooreian base of love and respect for the truth. His first few Apostles' papers were the work of an undergraduate in his early twenties, yet they always have dignity and sometimes an astonishing maturity.

As he was a meticulous craftsman and generous labourer, Strachey would prepare a large number of drafts of the pieces he intended for publication. Whole sections would be rewritten, new paragraphs inserted, and individual sentences and phrases lovingly polished and refined. But in the Apostles' papers – where there was seldom time for more than one draft – in his letters, and in a few unfinished pieces that exist only in first draft, there is a kind of freshness and spontaneous sparkle – the gift of the great conversationalist – that is not often present in his more polished work.

As an undergraduate Strachey had little interest in politics. The Boer War had been concluded and political discussion in the University centred on party politics, which did not greatly interest him. If at this time he had any concern for the great issue of socialism, it was a negative one. Though his brother James's undergraduate friends were to show strong sympathy for Fabianism, Lytton was unaffected by the movement and regarded Mrs Webb as rather a curiosity. He began to take an interest in conventional politics around 1909, but for Strachey, as for so many others of his generation, it was the coming of the Great War, and the introduction of conscription in 1916, that aroused in him lasting political interests. His attitude to the twin issues of the war and conscription is summed up in his statement of 7 March 1916 to the Hampstead Tribunal:

> I have a conscious objection to assisting, by any deliberate action of mine, in carrying on the war. This objection is not based on religious belief, but upon moral considerations, at which I arrived after long and careful thought. I do not wish to assert the extremely general proposition that I should never in any circumstances, be justified in taking part in any conceivable war; to dogmatize so absolutely upon a point so abstract would appear to me to be unreasonable. At the same time, my feeling is directed not simply against the present war: I am convinced that the whole system by which it is sought to settle international disputes by force is profoundly evil; and that, so far as I am concerned, I should be doing wrong to take any active part in it.
>
> These conclusions have crystallized in my mind since the outbreak of war. Before that time, I was principally occupied with literary and speculative matters; but, with the war, the supreme importance of international questions was forced upon my attention. My opinions in general have been for many years strongly critical of the whole structure of society; and, after a study of the diplomatic situation, and of the literature, both controversial and philosophical, arising out of the war, they developed naturally with those which I now hold. My convictions as to my duty with regard to the war have not been formed either rashly or lightly; and I shall not act against those convictions, whatever the consequences may be.

From his letters to James in the year 1916, we can see that he was faced with the problem posed today by the Vietnam war for many young Americans and Commonwealth citizens: how to claim exemption from war activities on grounds of conscientious objection, when the objection is to the injustice of a particular war, and not the absolute pacifist position of objecting to war as such. When Strachey answered the Tribunal's standard question, "What would you do if you saw a German soldier trying to rape your sister?" by saying, "I should attempt to come – [significant pause] – between them", it was not on grounds of pacifism, and the double entendre was intentional.

Like most artists at most times in history, Strachey was generally opposed to censorship. He was willing to defend indecency in art when it constituted a satisfactory part of a satisfying whole, and his thoughts on this subject, though one hesitates to claim originality for them, are expressed in a most refreshing manner. It must be said, however, that like many of his Bloomsbury friends, he was capable of a robust and wholehearted enjoyment of bawdiness in life, even if he thought it required some aesthetic justification in a work of art.

Strachey was well ahead of his time in his views on the role of women in society. His sister, Philippa, was very active in the women's suffrage movement, and had a long association with the feminist Fawcett Society. Strachey supported her struggles to get women the vote, and assisted her in Bertrand Russell's campaign to stand for Parliament in 1907 as a Suffragist. But his own views on the "woman question" went beyond giving women the vote; in several of his pieces he considers, sometimes explicitly, the whole question of sexual roles. It was clear to him, as it is to adherents of the various movements for the liberation of women, that the position of women depends, far more than on voting rights or than on educational opportunities, on the conception we have of the function of women, and on the feelings of both sexes about the appropriateness of their behaviour. Strachey fully realized that this conclusion entailed a searching look at the common notions of male behaviour. He had the courage of his homosexuality. But as the circumstances of his long association with the painter, Dora Carrington, make clear, Strachey relished the company of women, especially of emancipated ones, and although his sexual interests were directed principally towards men, he did acknowledge that the fact of gender is as important as the roles that society assigns to each of them. But just as he thought it natural for some people to be women, he thought it natural for some men, and for some women, to be homosexual. He never felt it necessary to make excuses for his own homosexuality, nor, like the militant homosexuals of a later age, did he regard a liking for one's own sex as a failure or an illness, or think it necessary or desirable to inquire into its origins. He was not shy of talking about his homosexuality, and enjoyed gossip about liaisons and intrigues, but openly, not furtively. To the Apostolic mind anything, even behaviour condemned by most of the world, was a fit subject for serious consideration, dignified discussion, and the exercise of humour. At a time when most of society found embarrassing even the mention of love outside the context of marriage and the family, Strachey could speak openly of his relationships not only to his friends but to his lovers themselves. He believed not only in sexual freedom, but in emotional freedom, and he bravely practised both.

In the pieces that follow, orthography and punctuation, both of which are often as eccentric as choice of vocabulary, have not been altered save in the case of obvious errors.

War and politics

COMMENTARY
1916 CORRESPONDENCE

The year 1916 was a watershed in Lytton Strachey's life. He was at work on the essays that were to become *Eminent Victorians*, his relationship with Dora Carrington was developing, and much of his private verse and prose was written in this year. But his chief concern was with the war and the introduction of conscription.

Many moderate people who favoured the war effort were reluctant to abandon Britain's non-conscriptionist tradition, as they felt that conscription savoured strongly of the militarism they believed themselves to be fighting. Strachey had little use for political moderation: he believed that the world was largely run by moderate men, that though the government of England and Germany were not composed of madmen, their policies none the less verged on lunacy. In an essay called "Militarism and Theology", which he published in *War and Peace* for May 1918, he argued that the most terrifying and bloodthirsty sort of militarism is perfectly acceptable to "the great mass of ordinary, stolid, humdrum, respectable persons" who remain "the dominating force in human affairs", and whose ideas determine the moderate position.

Strachey was correct to think that moderate opinion would come to favour conscription. The way was prepared by the Registration Act of 1915, which called for a national registration of all men between the ages of fifteen and sixty-five. At the time of its passage, the Act was intended solely as an instrument to be used in a manpower crisis. By the autumn of that year, of course, it was clear that the crisis had already been reached. On 5 October Lord Derby began, on behalf of the government, his infamous recruiting campaign designed to induce men who had not enlisted to do so on the condition that they would not be forced to serve before other men whose claims to exemption were weaker. This was meant to be a voluntary plan: men were to "attest", to agree to enlist whenever called upon to do so, but the obligation was to be moral, not legal. As James Strachey's own experience with his relation and employer on the *Spectator*, St Loe Strachey, showed, the Derby Scheme in fact led to blackmail and coercion. By December the scheme had failed, and at Christmas the government proposed to conscript all unmarried men under forty-five who were physically fit and not exempt on grounds that they did work of national importance or had exceptional domestic responsibilities.

By the spring of 1916 it was evident that even this measure was not enough, and by May the exemption of married men had to be ended. There was now general conscription, which moderate opinion had opposed only months before; but this measure and the one before it passed by large majorities, and there was virtually no organized opposition to their passage, in Parliament or in the country. The provisions made for conscientious objection were imprecise, and each claim for the status of conscientious objector had to be dealt with by a tribunal whose guidelines for granting exemptions were never clear, and whose procedures were unspecified. This was precisely the situation that obtained in the United States until the 1971 Supreme Court decision restricting conscientious objection to religious believers. It is ironical that it could easily have been Lytton Strachey who maintained that moderation in defence of liberty is no virtue.

By December of 1915 there was an urgent need for anti-conscription activity, and both Lytton and James Strachey immediately joined the No Conscription Fellowship, almost always referred to as the N.C.F., and the National Council against Conscription, the N.C.C. Both groups existed to resist the Act, and their activities were largely confined to the distribution of propaganda. Many members of Bloomsbury were among the stamp-stickers and envelope-sealers of the N.C.C., and Lytton even wrote a leaflet:

CONSCRIPTION
WHY they want it, and why they say they want it.

THEY SAY THEY WANT IT to punish the slackers
THEY WANT IT to punish the strikers.
THEY SAY THEY WANT IT to crush Germany
THEY WANT IT to crush labour.
THEY SAY THEY WANT IT to free Europe
THEY WANT IT to enslave England.
DON'T LET THEM GET WHAT THEY WANT BECAUSE THEY
KEEP SAYING THEY WANT SOMETHING DIFFERENT.

The Cat kept saying to the Mouse that she was a highminded person, and if the Mouse would only come a little nearer they could both get the cheese.

The Mouse said "Thank you, Pussy, it's not the cheese you want; it's my skin!"

Strachey's antipathy to H. W. Massingham, the editor of the *Nation*, probably sprang from an episode connected with this leaflet. Massingham got the point of the allegory, but decided it was seditious; he raced to the N.C.C. office to get the leaflet withdrawn from circulation. He was supported in this by Sir John Simon, the cabinet member who had resigned his post in order to lead the opposition to the Act, and it was decided to halt the distribution of the leaflet; Strachey thought this a cowardly decision, but as half a million copies were already in circulation he did not feel the need to register his disapproval too strongly.

The reader may detect some unflattering references to Maynard Keynes in these letters. Almost all Bloomsbury was of one mind about conscription and Keynes did refuse to attest under the Derby Scheme. But he also refused to resign his post at the Treasury unless universal conscription was introduced. It was introduced, but Keynes did not resign, much to the displeasure of Strachey and Bertrand Russell. Keynes said his sympathies lay with the conscientious objectors, and he was very effective in supporting the claims for exemption of James Strachey, Duncan Grant, and David Garnett. But his Bloomsbury friends felt there was an inconsistency in his sympathy for the objectors and his remaining at the Treasury where his job must have involved calculating the cheapest way to kill Germans. There was, in fact, some "pro-Germanism" in Bloomsbury; this did not consist in a denial of German belligerency or in an admiration of Prussian militarism, but in a vague fondness for the cultural achievements of the German people. Their objection to the "Kaiser War" was that the motives of both sides were ignoble.

At the time of writing Lytton Strachey was thirty-six years old, and James twenty-nine.

This selection includes most of the letters between Lytton and James Strachey for the year 1916. The few that have been omitted deal almost exclusively with domestic arrangements. The punctuation, sometimes eccentric, has not been altered.

1916 CORRESPONDENCE

In 1916 Lytton Strachey was frequently the guest of Lady Ottoline Morrell at her famous country house, Garsington Manor, near Oxford. Lady Ottoline (1873–1938), the half-sister of the Duke of Portland, never went to school, but was educated by her mother at Welbeck. Though not an intellectual herself, she was hostess and patroness to some of the most distinguished and talented people in England. Her circle included D. H. Lawrence, Yeats, Walter de la Mare, T. S. Eliot, Augustus John, Henry Lamb, the Stracheys, Virginia Woolf, Aldous Huxley, and Siegfried Sassoon. For a time she and Bertrand Russell were lovers.

"Pipsey" was her husband, Philip Edward Morrell (1870–1943), Liberal M.P. for South Oxfordshire (1906–10) and Burnley (1910–18). He shared his wife's aesthetic tastes and advanced social views. In 1913 the Morrells left London for Garsington. Both were strong pacifists and their home became a refuge for conscientious objectors, to whom they were very generous. In 1924 the Morrells returned to London, and their house at 10 Gower Street in Bloomsbury became the setting for Lady Ottoline's famous salon.

[postcard]
Garsington Manor
Oxford
Thursday

Her Ladyship says she would be charmed if you could come down any time next week, or the week-end following. No need to answer. I wonder if anything is happening. Pipsey's deputation

6

to the P.M. is this afternoon. It is very damp and grim down here, but peaceful.

Oh, do you happen to know the name of a Morris dance authority? (Either a book or a person.) O is getting up some dreadful village festivity, and has no idea how to instruct the children. 23 are coming today to be taught! – Frantic! – any information would be gratefully received.

Lytton

"Pippa" was Philippa Strachey (1872-1968), the third of the five Strachey sisters. A formidable lady with a great sense of humour, she was a crusader for women's rights, and was closely associated with the Fawcett Society.

Gerald Shove (1887–1947) whose name is best known to economists, was a pacifist and conscientious objector. He ran *War and Peace* for Norman Angell while waiting to be called up. His friendship with the Stracheys and with Rupert Brooke dated from his time as an undergraduate at Cambridge, where he was also an Apostle. He was married to the poet Fredegond Maitland.

Henry William Massingham (1860–1924) resigned the editorship of the *Daily Chronicle* in 1899 because of his opposition to the Boer War. As editor of the *Nation* from 1907 to 1923, he transformed this liberal weekly into a powerful organ of advanced but independent opinion; at the end of this period he joined the Labour Party and transferred his "Wayfarer's Diary" to the *New Statesman*. Massingham wavered in his feelings about the war, and had even supported it in its early stages.

John Atkinson Hobson (1858–1940) was an economist and publicist. He was a frequent contributor to the *Nation* when it was edited by Massingham. He had an original approach to economics which, though later praised by Keynes and Tawney as pioneering work, earned him the wrath of his colleagues to such an extent that he was never allowed to hold a university post. He was a founder of the Union of Democratic Control.

Lord Henry Cavendish-Bentinck was Lady Ottoline's brother. "Harold" was evidently the subject of one of Strachey's intrigues. There are references to him in later letters, one in connection with a visit from the police.

7

Garsington Manor
Oxford
Jan. 14th 1916

I had a most depressing conversation with Pippa before coming down here, in which she sketched the proper course of action for opposing the Bill; it seemed clearer than ever that the Reptiles in charge of the business were inconceivably incompetent. I departed in despair. But Philip now seems to think that it may take a fortnight or even three weeks getting through the Committee stage; and in that case isn't it still possible that something should be done? Surely there ought to be a continual stream of leaflets and pamphlets. Also if possible, meetings all over the country, and signatures collected against the Bill. Don't you think it might be worth while seeing Gerald, and if necessary supplanting him? He is clearly a mere blocade. But if you do anything, go and talk to Pippa first. Probably it's all pretty hopeless by this time, for *us* to try and intervene effectively; but the abomination of those Massingham–Hobson creatures makes one itch to. I am beginning to believe in Napoleon and Mr Lloyd George.

It is pretty dreary here – they're so stupid, so painfully stupid; but I suppose it's healthy. Huxley is just what you described. I really don't know what to say to him. The Lord Henry Cavendish-Bentinck arrives today. Did he see me last Saturday walking past his window with Harold?

Yours

Lytton

I return Monday or Tuesday.

This draft of James Strachey's statement to a Recruitment and Exemption Tribunal is written on the back of a No Conscription Fellowship circular which is dated 13 February 1916.

I conscientiously hold it to be wrong to take any part in the war; and my objection applies not only to combatant service but to any action which is likely to assist in its prosecution.

8

(As evidence that this opinion is genuinely held by me, I may perhaps mention the fact that last November I gave up a position which I had held for many years on the staff of the "Spectator" newspaper, rather than attest under Lord Derby's scheme, as I was requested to do by my employer.)

J.S.

Charles Edward Montague (1867–1928) was a journalist who had crusaded, with his paper, the *Manchester Guardian*, against the Boer War and for free trade, home rule, and nearly every liberal cause. But in 1914 he dyed his grey hair and enlisted as a private soldier. By the time of this letter he was serving in the intelligence service.

In his lifetime Lytton Strachey and his friends and relations were associated with at least eight houses in Gordon Square, Bloomsbury. But the reference in this letter must be to no. 46, the home of Clive and Vanessa Bell, where Duncan Grant, David Garnett ("Bunny"), and Maynard Keynes were often to be found.

This letter was written just over four months before Lord Kitchener's death by drowning. Keynes's gossip was largely correct and widely known; William Robertson (later knighted) had accepted the appointment as Chief of the Imperial General Staff in December 1915, on condition that a small War Council to coordinate strategy in all war theatres was formed with himself as its military adviser in direct touch with his commanders without intervention of the Army Council; he also demanded a reorganization of the General Staff in the War Office. Robertson was the first general in history to have come up through the ranks; his accent was certainly an unusual one for the C.I.G.S., but it was not strictly accurate to call him "our Cockney General".

On 2 February 1916 James had written, à propos of the new translation of Dostoyevsky's *A Raw Youth*: "I note that Mrs Garnett has invented a new exclamation. Not only Ach! and Ech! but now Och!"

6 Belsize Park Gardens
Hampstead, N.W.
Feb. 22nd 1916

It's all terribly bleak in every direction. I'm glad you're going to Burley, perhaps by then things will improve.

The man at Bicken assured me with such complete conviction that the *Raw Youth* was not yet out that I believed him, luckily. I'm looking forward to it. I'm now half way through Foma Formitch.

Do you really want the *M. Guardian* a day late? I suppose you realise it will be that, and so – I'll order it.

I cut out the *Observer* report of Montague's speech (it had *every* horror, not only protection but the necessity for smashing Germany etc.) and wrote on a piece of notepaper the following – "Dear Maynard, why are you still in the Treasury? Yours, Lytton." I was going to post it to him, but he happened to be dining at Gordon Square where I also was. So I put the letter on his plate. He really *was* rather put out when he read the extract. He said that two days before he had had a long conversation with Montague in which that personage had talked violently in exactly the opposite way. He said the explanation was cowardice. I said that if their cowardice went as far as that there was no hope. And what was the use of his going on imagining he was doing any good with such people? I went on for a long time with considerable virulence, Nessa, Duncan and Bunny sitting round in approving silence. (Luckily Clive wasn't there.) The poor fellow seemed very decent about it, and admitted that *part* of his reason for staying was the pleasure he got from his being able to do the work so well. He also seemed to think he was doing a great service to the country by saving some millions per week. I maintained that that sort of thing was mere fiddle-faddle, and that the really important things were the main principles, such as Free Trade, over which he had no control whatever. He at last admitted that there *was* a point at which he *would* think it necessary to leave, but what that point might be he couldn't say.

He had a little gossip – (1) that the other day the French made a frantic effort to involve us at once in a grand Ally Protection scheme, and that this would probably have been done, if he hadn't written an unbridled minute. And (2) that K. is now a mere dummy, everything of importance being done, and signed, by Robertson (our Cockney General). He told a story about him in France, when it became necessary to get rid of several French liaison officers, and nobody knew how to dismiss them tactfully. At last Robertson was asked to see to it, as he had such a reputation for diplomacy. So he said he would, and summoned the

French officers to meet him. They all appeared, were put to sit round a table, and Robertson sat at the head. He then slowly pointed his finger at each of them one after the other, saying, with every point, "*You* go 'ome", "*you* go 'ome." – And 'ome they went!

My health is still far from satisfactory. It is horribly cold here, and I feel chilled to the bone. I have fearful nights too. Well! The Lord save us. Ach! Ech! Och!

Yours

Lytton

Burley Hill in the New Forest was the home of Thena Clough, who regularly lent it to members of the Strachey family. Roger Fry (1866–1934), the great art critic, was a member of Bloomsbury and an Apostle of a rather older generation than James and Lytton. Robert Threshie Reid, Earl Loreburn (1846–1923) had been Lord Chancellor until 1912. He retired to Dover, but in January 1918 returned to London to lead the deputation commending Lord Lansdowne for his courage in attempting to counter the vicious propaganda circulating internally both in Britain and in Germany, which the veteran Lord Lansdowne felt was prolonging the war. (Joan) Pernel Strachey (1876–1951), another of the remarkable Strachey sisters, was principal of Newnham College from 1923–41. The "Old Man" was the nickname, not always used with affection, of the then Prime Minister, Asquith.

Burley Hill
Ringwood
Feb. 24 1916

Thursday evening

We've just arrived here, having been put off for a day by Pippa, apparently because Roger was stopping on. We met him for a second at the station, and he pressed a packet of Velma into our hands.

This is more civilized; but the arctic conditions continue.

I sent in my application on Tuesday, the day before the crowd, as I gathered from the *M.G.* I went in only for conscience; just said I thought the war wrong and wouldn't do anything of any kind to help in it; and added "as evidence that I genuinely hold this view" the fact of my leaving the *Spec*.

I now think that all is lost; I feel sure from studying the papers that at the most they'll put you in Class 4 and exempt me from combatant service. On the other hand I now envisage prison and even execution fairly calmly, chiefly because I've been reading *The Times* for the last half-hour.

I note another thing as to you. It looks to me as though the tribunals were absolutely refusing (illegally?) to exempt *anyone* on medical grounds. That's to say they prefer to leave the decision to the military authorities. In that case you'ld be "called up" and be examined *after* you'd been "deemed". This complicates things extremely, expecially in connection with "conscience". Are you preparing a short "statement" to read out to the Tribunal? It seems to me that might be wise.

I can't make anything of the Race Debate, it's so badly reported. But that Old Man seems to me appallingly wicked.

Lord Loreburn was very dashing again yesterday.

Yours

James

Pernel seems to be stopping here after all.

Charles à Court Repington (1858–1925) had to abandon his brilliant military career in 1902 as a result of an indiscretion committed with the wife of a British official in Egypt. Forced to resign his commission, he was refused a divorce by his wife, and was unable to make amends to the lady whose position he had compromised. He became the military correspondent of *The Times* in 1904, and served on Recruiting and Exemption Tribunals from 1914 to 1918. The two books of reminiscences he published after the war (to revive his ailing financial situation) revealed so much private information and caused such scandal that Repington again lost his social position. He did, however, achieve a reconciliation with his wife shortly before his death.

C. P. Sanger (1871–1930) excelled as barrister, economist and literary critic. He was strongly opposed to the war and was a great admirer of German culture.

Adrian Stephen was one of the sons of Sir Leslie Stephen, and brother of Virginia Woolf and Vanessa Bell. In 1910 he and Horace Cole were the chief perpetrators of the great *Dreadnought* hoax. A party which included Virginia and Duncan Grant, disguised as the Emperor of Abyssinia and his entourage, fooled the Royal Navy into conducting them aboard their latest ship, the *Dreadnought*, and explaining to them its mysteries. Stephen and Cole had earlier thought of masquerading as German officers and escorting a platoon across the Alsace-Lorraine frontier. Stephen studied law for a time, but later became a psycho-analyst, as did his wife, Karin Costelloe.

Beatrice Chamberlain (1862–1918) was the eldest daughter of Joseph Chamberlain. She had been a childhood friend of Lytton Strachey.

Mary Hutchinson, the wife of St John Hutchinson, is a cousin of the Stracheys. She was very close to Lytton Strachey in the last years of his life. At the time of writing she was an art student at the Slade.

Burley Hill
Ringwood
Feb. 26th 1916

Thanks for the various documents. Colonel Henderson was or is, I fancy, Lord Derby's private secretary in his capacity of Director-General of Recruiting. How can one discover? I think the remark makes a very good admission for purposes of arguing with the tribunal. I'll keep the number containing it.

Sir John's speech seemed very well done; but the subject isn't perhaps very interesting.

By the way, there's only one post here per diem (owing to war economy), and you can't be certain of catching it unless you post very early. (The ordinary 5.30 from London has missed it 2 or 3 times.) And then it doesn't arrive till two days after.

The ladies here (Pippa at all events) don't seem to me to appre-ciate the position of things. She announced ex cathedra that you really hadn't any conscientious objection, and that you oughtn't to have said you had – repeating very much the sort of thing she said in her letter. I tried to explain what I thought were the facts – but she seemed adherent [sic]. At the same time she was violently anti-conscription – and possibly more. I think she thinks you can only have a "conscientious" objection if it's to "war in general" or "taking human life" – in fact if it's an unreasonable objection. I fancy the tribunal may take the same view.

13

I am intending at present to return on Thursday or Friday – stop one night – and go away again for the week-end.

There's about a foot of snow, so movement is difficult.

I was asked last night by sudden telegram to H.G.'s for the week-end. I'm rather sorry to have had to miss it.

Yours

James

6 *B.P.G.*
Feb. 28th 1916

I wish you could induce Pippa to realize the gravity of the situation. It also worries me to think that she considers me either a humbug or a dunderhead. The conscience question is very difficult and complicated, and no doubt I have many feelings against joining the army which are not conscientious; but *one* of my feelings is that if I were to find myself doing clerical work in Class IVb – i.e. devoting all my working energy to helping in the war – I should be doing wrong; I should be convinced that I was doing wrong the whole time; and if that isn't having a conscientious objection I don't know what is. If she doesn't believe me when I say this I'm sorry, but I suppose she won't believe me any more if I add that I'm willing to go to prison rather than do that work. I'm afraid she may not have considered what that means. I have. I don't suppose I shall go to prison, but if they insist I am ready for it. Well! I must say it adds to the disagreableness of things if one's to find that Pippa doesn't give one her support.

I'm glad to say I'm feeling much better – in fact almost normal. I only hope it'll last. I hope you've pretty well recovered by this time. The nervous strain of the tribunal hanging over one's head is getting rather intense, I find. Nothing has come from them. I'm told by Bunny that Colonel Repington is on the Hampstead tribunal (not as military representative) – it sounds quite likely. I think it quite possible that they may take up the same sort of view about conscience as Pippa – viz. that the act does not provide for conscientious objection against this war, but only for some flummery against war in general. I shall consult Sanger about this, as I gather he's up in it all. I am quite ready if necessary to tell any number of lies – *if necessary*. But I shall tell them with my eyes open. Footpads! Footpads at the street corner! Knock them down if you can, but if you can't cut and run!

Adrian has been watching the St Pancras tribunal (Duncan's and Bunny's) and reports darkly. He says it's entirely dominated by the military representative and one or two loud-voiced hooligans; that there are decent people on it, but that they're terrified and powerless. The amount of appalling and senseless misery caused by the act makes one's blood run cold to think of. I really think that that poor woman with her Jesus and her hysteria who was sent to gaol for 6 months on Saturday is nearer the Kingdom of Heaven than most of us. To have devoted her whole time since the beginning of the war to discouraging recruiting! It is wonderful that such people should exist.

I had rather an odd conversation yesterday with my old friend, Beatrice Chamberlain. She asked me to dinner by telephone. I felt, all things considered, that I couldn't stand it, so said I was engaged. She then asked me to come to tea on Sunday, and I said I would. We were tête-à-tête and, as a good opening offered, I thought it as well to explain the nature of my opinions: it seemed silly going on indefinitely with the poor woman in the dark. She was very calm, and we talked hard for an hour and a half. It was almost entirely about the justification of the war; the conscription business was just *effleuré*, but it gets me so much on the raw that I thought it better to glissade away from that. Rather a pity perhaps, as her *great* reason for wanting to smash Germany (or so she said) was her love of freedom. She was very adroit, especially in the *technique* of argument – viz. skimming over difficult places, and the rest of it – but some of her arguments were curiously childish. Such is my well-known fair-mindedness that I saw a good deal in her position, but on the other hand nothing I said, I'm sure, had the slightest effect on her – not the very slightest. She didn't budge by a pin's point. I pressed her to give some account of how she thought we should win. (She had said she was *perfectly certain* that we should.) After a little prevarication she admitted that the West was jammed. I then said "Well then how are we to do it?" She replied "There may be other ways." I said "What?" And she answered "Roumania may join us. I don't say she will, but she may." And that was all she had to offer. I said that it seemed to me

15

she was not using her reason on this matter, and she as good as confessed that she wasn't. "You underrate the power of character in getting things done", etc. I thought there was something to be said for that; but time will show. I then elicited, bit by bit, the terms that would satisfy her. They were as follows – a *complete* indemnity for Belgium (also Serbia), Alsace Lorraine for France, German Poland to join Russian Poland under Russia, and Galitia to join too if it wants to (ahem!), Constantinople to Russia, and all German colonies kept. (I forgot to ask about Italy.) This I gathered was a minimum. It seems to me to throw rather a lurid light on the state of mind of the moderate Tories. She sat there talking like that, with Verdun (as she admitted) tottering... At last I went, and we parted on friendly terms. But I don't think I shall be seen there again. Personally, she didn't come well out of the conversation. I do not care for her, no. She has no feelings – she once had – for "Papa", but they lie buried in his grave, and now her heart is a piece of dried seaweed. One detail was instructive. I said that I supposed she intended to keep Mesopotamia; upon which she hummed and hawed, and at last said "there are difficulties about Mesopotamia". Considering her family connection with India, I think this must mean something – probably that the Russians have signified that we must keep our hands off. But if so, is it possible to imagine a more ghastly nightmare of folly than that expedition?

I feel there must be many more things to say, but this letter is already inordinate, and I have to go to lunch with Mary Hutchinson. Oh! I finished off Miss Lowell t'other day – very nasty I was; so now I've only H.W. to be done in 3 weeks – shall I live through it? I'll write again soon. What a pity to miss H.G.!

Yours

Lytton

"Je meurs pour ne point faire un aveu si funeste." – What would the redoubtable Repington say to that?

Ray Strachey *née* Costelloe (1887–1940) was married to James and Lytton Strachey's brother Oliver, and was the sister of Adrian Stephen's wife Karin. She was a leading figure in the women's rights movement. Marjorie Strachey (1882–1964) was the youngest sister. "Pa Scott" was C. P. Scott (1846–1932), the celebrated editor of the *Manchester Guardian*.

"Mardle" refers to a note from a servant.

Henry Tertius James Norton (1887–1936) was a rather less famous member of the Bloomsbury group. A fellow-Apostle, conscientious objector, and great friend of the Stracheys, Harry Norton did ground-breaking work on the mathematical theory of genetics, but died relatively unknown.

Noel Olivier was one of the talented daughters of Lord Olivier, the first socialist peer. A medical student during the war, she was a close friend of James Strachey and Rupert Brooke.

6 B.P.G.
Feb. 29th 1916

I saw Ray last night, who said she had been to Manchester and seen Marjorie, who reported an interview she had had with Pa Scott: I gather he said that he intended to have you – when the exemption question was cleared up; also that the work he had in mind was piece work – not a place on the staff with a definite salary, and that it would involve living in Manchester. As all this comes through 2 people it may be incorrect in details, but I suppose the main outlines are true. I think Marjorie might have written to you about it, but I don't suppose she has. It seems to me rather mean of Pa not to have you at once, if he's going to at all, because your position *vis-à-vis* to the tribunal would probably be better if you were working for him than if you were doing nothing. However, I suppose he doesn't want an indefinite arrangement.

I think that if Pa should break down something really might be done with Massingham.

Tonight I dine with Sanger (after Bertie on Religion) and hope to glean some advice.

A propos of Verdun, Beatrice had been informed by some French personage of importance that the German guns were larger than the French, and that this was the cause of their success. She seemed quite prepared for its fall – but this of course was 2 days back.

I enclose Mardle.

Yours

Lytton

Monday morning

I opened most of your letters in case action was necessary.

I'm summoned for Thursday also: but at 6.30. The short-hand report seems to have got 85% of the words wrong.

I suppose you've heard that Norton's got off altogether.

You'll find last Thursday's H. of C. most interesting. Note Mr Hogge's question; – I've turned down the page. Tennant seemed to disgrace himself badly at midnight, and Mr Outhwaite was rather fine.

Back to dinner.

J.

Noel suggests it might be a good plan to try and get some more *technical* statement out of Overy, for showing to *doctors* – who are less likely to be impressed by a popular testimonial.

I think we may be on the telephone today.

The Strachey's "pro-Germanism" did not, of course, extend to approval of Germany's conduct of the war.

Sir Edward Fry (1829–1918), a noted judge, was a strong Quaker. He was the father of Roger Fry. Lord Parmoor, formerly Charles Alfred Cripps (1852–1941), lawyer and politician, was a pacifist and became interested in the League of Nations. "Our brother J. G. Butcher" is a private joke. The J. G. Butcher who participated in the correspondence in *The Times* was Major-General Sir George James Butcher (1860–1939), D.D.O.S. Woolwich throughout the war. The Apostolic J. G. Butcher was the less war-like Lord Danesfort (1853–1935), an eminent barrister and scientist.

"Connie" was Constance Garnett (1862–1946), the translator of the whole of the works of Turgenev, Dostoyevsky, Gogol, nearly all of Chekhov, and Tolstoy's two novels. James uses her Christian name because she was the mother of Bunny Garnett.

Burley Hill
March 1st 1916

There's a letter from Colonel Repington in *The Times* today, saying that he's on a tribunal – so I suppose the story's true.

I incline to think it might actually be good policy to say the truth, viz. that one's objection is to *this* war. It seems to me clear that the words of the Act ("conscientious objection to combatant service") cover us. They say nothing as to the *motive* of the objection – whether it's due to a general regard for the sanctity of human life, or to more particular objections to combatant service at the present moment – so long as the motive is "conscientious". That word gives opportunities for endless argument; and it seems to me that, if they refuse exemption, there'ld be a good chance of carrying up an appeal to the Central Tribunal on the purely legal point. But it also seems to me that though one's objection to the present war (one's pro-Germanism) will infuriate the tribunals far more than mere Tolstoyism, they'll be most likely to think "We don't want fellows like that in the Army". – But I see that even so they may put one down for Class IVb.

Have you got the following documents?:

(1) Mr Long's Instructions.
(2) Mr Long's Recommendations.

(These two are different. But I don't know their exact names. The first is, I suppose, an Order in Council.)

Would it be possible to find, do you think, a quotation from some Militarist authority saying that the Medical and Sanitary branches of a modern army are as vital to its action as the combatant? If we could get such a quotation from Rep. himself it would be effective: but I don't see how it's to be done. And anything else like Colonel Henderson's admission about Clerks.

I hope the reports of the Debate are still being kept. We must go through the parts on Con. Ob. again carefully.

Wouldn't it be useful to go and "watch" one day, to grasp the procedure. I'm so doubtful whether we shall get any chance of stating our position at all.

The morning post's going. I'll continue later.

I've got all your letters down to Pa Scott.
Have *you* had a Yellow Form?

Yours

James

Burley Hill
March 1st
6 p.m.

I think you should take in *The Times*. In spite of its horrors, it has points of interest, especially in the letters. There's been a correspondence on Habeas Corpus, with Sir E. Fry and Lord Parmoor on one side, and our brother J. G. Butcher on the other.

I enclose the Colonel's letter today. Its tone seems to me the limit of insolence. And all it comes to is that he's just discovered that Sir John was right, and that when all exemptions have been made there are only a negligible quantity of single men left. I nearly wrote off to say so.

He also had a wildly hysterical article the day before yesterday; saying that he could at last reveal (what he's known from secret sources for many days) that the crisis of the war had arrived. The Verdun attack was only a preliminary; the main German attack would shortly be delivered elsewhere, probably in Champagne. A hundred and thirty divisions were now in the West; numbers of big guns had been brought across from Russia and Servia. The Kaiser was at Mézières at G.H.Q. Moreover Prince Henry of Prussia had been given command of the Fleet, which might be expected to come out at any moment. Preliminary mine-laying by submarines had already begun. These signs, and certain others even more weighty which he could not yet mention, proved that Germany was making her last gambler's throw.

I don't much expect myself that the Germans are going to do any good by this attack, even if they get Verdun. If it's true that the French haven't even yet got proper guns, I really think they deserve to be removed.

It sounds rather unsatisfactory about Manchester. Piece-work? But will he guarantee me a minimum?

I finished the *Raw Youth* the other day. The plot seemed more

20

disjointed than usual; in fact there are two utterly disconnected ones. But he's a most surprising writer, By God. – There's more than a touch or two of sodomy. And I also suspect Connie of leaving things out; though she bravely faces: "I can't think why I'm in such a bad temper today: I put it all down to haemorrhoids." Was that in the French?

Yours

James

Strachey's chief concern in March was his appearance before the Hampstead Tribunal, where he intended to claim an absolute exemption from military service on grounds of conscientious objection. He had first to appear before the local Advisory Committee, who summoned him on 7 March. Though nominally only advisory, the recommendations of the committees were invariably followed by the tribunals. Strachey read his prepared statement to the committee, who made no comment at all, and simply informed him that they would recommend that the tribunal afford him "no relief". He felt he would get no better hearing from the tribunal itself, but he was prepared to create a stir anyway, and spent his time, as he wrote to James, constructing "imaginary cross-examinations of Military Representatives".

The tribunal heard Strachey's case at the Town Hall on 17 March. The audience included Philip Morrell, his chief character witness, a host of brothers and sisters, and much of Bloomsbury. There followed the legendary scene with the pale-blue air cushion, solemnly handed by Morrell to Strachey, who inflated it, and, with a grave expression on his face, inserted it between himself and the bench. He was suffering from piles. The audience was delighted by this and by the famous repartee concerning German soldiers and sisters (see p. xiii), but the members of the tribunal were not much impressed. They adjourned the proceedings to await the report of the physical examination by the military doctors. The examination, held a few days later at the White City, was a greater success. Strachey was pronounced unfit for any kind of service.

John St Loe Strachey (1860–1927) was the conservative proprietor and editor of the *Spectator*. He had given employment to his cousin James Strachey, but sacked him when he refused the militaristic St Loe's demand that he attest under the Derby Scheme.

[*1916*]

Will you look at this, and if you think it any good, and have the strength to reach the post-box, will you address it and post it? My brain spins round and round.

G.L.S.

I appeal against the decision of the Hampstead Local Tribunal to refuse my claim for a certificate of absolute exemption from combatant service only on the grounds

(1) That the Tribunal refused to give any reason for their decision. (2) That their decision was unreasonable and not in accordance with the weight of evidence. I claimed exemption on the ground of an objection to the undertaking of combatant service and explained in my evidence that this objection was rested principally on an objection to taking any part whatever, direct or indirect, in the present war. The Tribunal stated repeatedly during the hearing that they accepted absolutely the veracity of my evidence and the honesty of my beliefs. The Military Representative stated in reply to a question that the ground upon which he resisted my claim was that my objection was not a "conscientious" one within the meaning of the Act. It is clear from the fact that the Tribunal granted me an exemption that they did not accept this view. Since, therefore, the Tribunal accepted my objection as being a conscientious one, and also accepted the veracity of my evidence as to the grounds of my objection, I claim that it was unreasonable of them to withhold from me the only form of exemption which would appropriately meet my objection. If my objection to the undertaking of combatant service had rested upon such grounds as a feeling that human life was sacred, it might have been reasonable to grant me exemption from combatant service only. But since my objection admittedly rested upon an objection to taking any part, direct or indirect, in the present war, the only exemption which could reasonably have been granted was an absolute one. (3) That the Tribunal refused to me my right under the Act to put relevant questions to the Military Representative (Regulations, Part I, Section I, Sub-sections 9 and 16c). The Chairman after a discussion said he did not admit my right, but would let me put questions as a matter of courtesy. The Military Representative

declined to answer my third question; whereupon the Chairman refused to let me press it, and again reminded me that I was putting the questions not as a right but as a matter of courtesy. I was consequently obliged to abandon any attempt to put further questions, though they were of the greatest importance to the complete statement of my claim.

[11 March 1916]
6 B.P.G. Sat.

I have received a summons to the tribunal for next Thursday 5 p.m. No other news, I think. You saw Ma's kind reference? "Bearing a well-known name" – I think it must be a dig at St Loe.

This it is hoped will reach you Monday morning. I wonder when you'll return. I fear the weather's hardly the thing for the South Downs.

I spend my days drawing up imaginary cross-examinations of Military Representatives.

Yr

Lytton

[Telegram]
Strachey 22 Brides Lane EC

Unfit for any class   *Lytton*

J. A. Hobson was evidently not of the opinion of Massingham that Lytton's "Pussy" – his circular for the N.C.C. denouncing the war – was seditious.

Clifford Allen (1889–1939) was created Baron Allen of Hurtwood in the last year of his life. He was an extremely courageous conscientious objector who was imprisoned three times in the course of the war. Lord Courtney (1832–1918) was a journalist and statesman, professor of political economy, and Liberal M.P. He was anti-imperialist and strongly favoured proportional representation.

I'm going to bring Noel back to dinner. Shall you be in? I met Prof. Hobson last night; he was most affable about your Pussy, and said he would speak to Pa Scott about me when he goes to Manchester next week-end.

J.

6 B.P.G.
March 29th 1916

Norton got a letter this morning to announce that the Military Representative has appealed against his exemption! He's now plunged in gloom, and feels convinced we shall all end our days in the Tower.

I had a long conversation today with Mr Clifford Allen, who was most gracious. They decided unanimously at their Executive on Saturday to refuse any compromise. I gather that the Quakers were represented at the meeting as well as the N.C.F. Lord Courtney is understood to be grieved at the decision. The government's proposals were practically what I told you: that an Order in Council should be made to the effect that the present occupation of all C.O.s was of national importance, and that they were all exempted from the Act on condition they continued in it. There was to be a Black List of trades, fixed by a committee; and any one in a Black List trade was to be draughted out into another. The Committee was to have representatives from the various conscientiously objecting bodies.

Apparently they haven't yet actually had a conference with any cabinet ministers; but they've got an appointment now with Mr Lloyd George as soon as he gets back from Paris – on Saturday, I think he said, or Monday. Mr Allen and one other person are to go and announce their decision to him; so I suppose it ought to be kept dark till then – though nothing was said on that score. I now begin to have qualms. Mr Allen seemed slightly *tête montée*, and talked of having the government on the run and of their being compelled to amend the Act. It seems to me a little soon to say that. However on the whole he was sensible and apparently saw that even if we succeed it'll only be after a good deal of individual suffering. – They haven't, as far as is known, yet arrested any N.C.F. member; but there are dark rumours of the suicide of 2 extraneous persons after they had been four days in the hands of the military. – Meanwhile an extremely influentially signed petition is being prepared for the Old Man – signed, in fact, by Lord Courtney, the Bishop of Oxford, Mrs Creighton, and Mr Massingham – begging the government to abstain from any prosecutions of C.O.s until the question has been more cleared up, and also, I think, pointing out how un-uniformly the law has been administered.

It is generally thought, I can't make out why, that the government is tottering and will fall within the next fortnight or 3 weeks. Unless the Peace Conference has come to anything. We are informed on good authority that it *was* a Peace Conference: that Colonel House's terms offered by Germany were genuine, and that they've been considering them in Paris. (Has Perrier Jouet gone to Rome to interview the Pope?) Can one believe that sort of thing?

The grand National Conference of the N.C.F. takes place on Saturday week: – a thousand delegates from all parts of the kingdom. There's to be an afternoon demonstration to which the Press and Scotland Yard will be invited – with many extremely influential people on the platform – in fact, Lord Courtney, the Bishop of Oxford, Mrs Creighton, and Mr Massingham. Mr Allen has most graciously promised me a ticket.

My Executive yesterday was duller than ever. Harry and Mr Lansbury (a nice man) were there. Harry is secretary to the legal sub-committee, and is supposed to be getting up a case for an application in the Divisional Court for a writ of *certiorari*. It came out that Lord Parmoor hopes to arrange for a debate in the House of Lords, and has promised to approach various other Lords: Morley, Loreburn, Courtney, the Bishop of Oxford, Mrs Creighton, and Mr Massingham.

I think those are the main points. I havn't gone to Mrs Hutch's party tonight, because I'm really too sleepy.

Yours

James

No rumours from Glasgow; but I should think the government are likely to hash things there.

Edward Henry, Baron Carson (1854–1935) was the Ulster leader who was Attorney-General from May 1915 to October 1916. He was dissatisfied about the delay in applying conscription.

Duncan Grant had rented Wissett Lodge to establish himself and David Garnett as official fruit-farmers in order to satisfy their obligations under the National Service Act. Vanessa Bell was frequently at Wissett Lodge.

"Bob Trevy" was R. C. Trevelyan (1872–1951), the poet. He was an Apostle, as was his brother, the historian G. M. Trevelyan.

Asheham was the Sussex home of Leonard and Virginia Woolf. Faith Bagenal, later Henderson, had recently come down from Newnham College.

> *Garsington Manor*
> *Oxford*
> *March 30th 1916*

I was very glad to get your letter. It is too sickening about Norton. I hope he's not *abruti*.

The N.C.F. position sounds exciting. It seems to me that Clifford Allen's line is decidedly extremist, if the government has really offered what you say. But it's difficult to say that he's not right. Probably the extremity of extremism is the best thing now. Bertie, I gather, is coming to London on purpose to help the N.C.F. It might be a good thing to get a sight of him.

Philip had heard nothing of the rumour that the Paris meeting was a Peace one. He said that the general impression before yesterday was that the government, or at any rate Asquith, was done for; but that after Carson's speech yesterday, which was a complete frost, everyone agreed that things would go on as before.

It seems to me that if the government has a grain of sense it will make peace as soon as it can, as that's the only way of getting out of all their difficulties.

I wonder how the domestic affairs are proceeding. I've heard from Pippa that her disease has broken out again in a new form, which is very sickening. I am feeling very comfortable and cheerful, but still exceedingly exhausted. I hope before long this will stop.

Ott. suggested that you should come down the Sat. after next. I told her I didn't know what your plans are.

Yours

Lytton

Philip complains that in spite of his prayers he was only given *one* question by Mr Backhouse – said he would have liked to ask at least ½ a dozen. I suppose there must be material for endless questions, and it seems a mistake not to use it as much as possible.

> *Garsington*
> *March 31st 1916*

The more I think of it, the more certain I feel that the N.C.F. is right in refusing to compromise. If conscientious objectors once begin to allow themselves to be put into occupations by the government, they are done for. The duty of the government is quite clear – viz. to see that the Act is properly carried out, and that the "out-and-out" C.O.s are given absolute exemption. There's really no reason on earth why they shouldn't be. And I expect it could be quite easily arranged by an Order in Council – if it's true that the government's compromise could be. No doubt an amendment to the Act is out of the question.

If you see Mr Allen again, I beg you to encourage him.

God blast, confound, and fuck the Upper Classes.

Yours

Lytton

> [postcard]
> *19 Marlborough Road, N.W.*
> *Friday night*

I expect you'll have heard of the Duncan fiasco – that his case, after the usual audience had collected, was transferred to the Wissett Rural District Local Tribunal.

I'm going to Bob Trevy's for the week-end. Back on Monday.

J.

Garsington Manor
Oxford
Sat. Apr. 15th 1916

I shall return for Tuesday night, going to Asheham on Thursday. Are you going to the M.F. on Tuesday? I am going with Faith, etc. I don't know about dinner. I should think the best thing would be to have it in Town.

I'm still feeling rather a wraith, I'm sorry to say. The news seems utterly revolting – these appalling imprisonments. Bertie is expected today, and perhaps Clifford Allen.

Yr

Lytton

Philip Snowden (later Viscount Snowden) (1864–1937) led the minority of the Labour movement who opposed the war. A brave champion of conscientious objectors, his unpopular opinions lost him his seat in Parliament in 1918.

Gilbert Cannan (1884–1955) was a minor novelist whose *Mendel*, published in the year this letter was written, contained a thinly disguised portrait of Lytton's friend Dora Carrington.

Walter Hume Long, later Viscount Long of Wraxall (1854–1924), was the cabinet member responsible for framing the conscription acts in the 1915 Coalition Government.

Barbara Bagenal, then Barbara Hiles, was then a Slade student.

6, B.P.G.
April 4th 1916

Goodness. What a life!

I'd just finished a solitary dinner five minutes ago and had dropped for a moment into the W.C. when I heard a ring at the front door. A good deal of inquiring seemed to be going on, and when I came out in a minute or two, there I saw, standing in the hall by the front door, the stately figures of two police constables. I naturally jumped to the conclusion that I was going to spend the night in gaol, so you can imagine that I was feeling rather agitated when I went up to them and asked if I could do anything for them. "Well, sir," said one of them, infinitely polite and kindly, "we've come to ask if Mr Giles Lytton Strachey lives here." "He usually lives here; – but I'm afraid he's away at present ..." "I see, sir. The fact is, sir, the Military Authorities have been making some inquiries about him; so we just called round to see him." "I could give you his address, if that would be any good to you." "Thank you very much, sir." "Care of Lady Ottoline O double-T O LINE Morrell ..." etcetera. "Thank you, sir. Stopping away for his health?" (Had they got this out of Jessie?) "Yes." "I see. (Making a note.) Stopping away indefinitely for the benefit of his health. – And you're his brother, sir?" "Yes. Mr *James* Strachey." "Thank you, sir. Then they'll be able to get in touch with him there if necessary?" "Yes." "Goodnight, sir." "Goodnight."

I can still hardly get over it. Have the Military Authorities simply not realized that you've been exempted? And if you'd been here would you have been waltzed off to the Police Station? ... It occurred to me for a moment that it might be something quite different. ... Harold ... but they mentioned the Military Authorities all right.

The week-end was rather pleasant.

No particular news. I expect you've heard that Snowden's to raise the question of the behaviour of Appeal Tribunals (a sort of continuation of his last speech) on the adjournment on Thursday. If there's time, Philip's to speak as well, as a rejoinder to any official reply. (Will you say, by the way, that I made a speech at the Executive today about giving him questions to ask? I think it may have some effect.) There's also to be a House of Lords debate shortly.

Norton seems to be giving up and returning to Cambridge tomorrow. His place is to be taken by – Gilbert Cannan – who is also to act as understudy to me. I find him fearfully hard to deal with – gloomy, speechless, and *not* very clever. ... But then even Bertie this morning failed to understand that paragraph in Mr Long's new circular, till I'd explained it to him.

Yours

James

Garsington Manor
Oxford
Ap. 5th 1916

Very odd – the dear Bobbies. You don't say whether they were good looking; but I'm told the one here *is*, so perhaps if he does get "in touch" with me. . . . And then there's "Harold" – but I suppose I can depend on the Military Authorities. Queer that one should positively fall back on *them* with relief. The worst of it is that when these things begin one never knows where they mayn't end; perhaps it's also the best of it.

I think probably it's the result of the Yellow Form, which I daresay called me up on Ap. 4th – and I paid no attention to it. Nor have I got any papers here of any sort: all those dealing with that question (including the Registration card) I left in that right-hand drawer. If you think it wise, will you send me whatever you think I ought to have? (Heavily registered) – But perhaps really they won't take any more steps about it. And ought I to do anything with the Yellow Form? Rather late in the day, I should think.

Gilbert C. sounds a very dismal office companion. You'll never make him understand an Act of Parliament. I'm glad there's to be another debate, and I hope Pipsey will figure. He is so earnest.

I am getting on here quite satisfactorily – everything flows along in a comfortable way, though to be sure the week-end *was* rather a hurricane. But that only lasted for a day and a half, and otherwise I've done nothing but sleep, eat, and read Prof. Gardner. I don't think there'll be anyone besides you next Saturday – it seemed on the whole best, so I didn't encourage other invitations. My health seems better, but the exhaustion is still rather great. I hope you're not absolutely dropping. And your Appeal?

I heard from Barbara about Duncan's affair. The prospect of the Suffolk Appeal Tribunal is I fear rather black. But Something, I presume, before then is bound to happen.

I think it would be madness to rush up on Saturday for the N.C.F. meeting, much as I should like it. I think I'll try and write them a few words of encouragement. But my invitation wasn't signed, so I hardly know who to address it to.

I've been spending the afternoon in Oxford, lingering among those mouse-eaten buildings, and trying to get up a few romantic memories. But really I couldn't; the streets were so full of soldiers that my attention was distracted; and I found that I was thinking of the Present and the Future, and not of the Past.

Yours

Lytton

Goldsworthy Lowes Dickinson (1862–1932) was a philosopher at Cambridge. He was fiercely opposed to the war, but directed his energies chiefly to planning for the peace to follow, and was a leading figure in the founding of the League of Nations. He was an Apostle and a great influence on many members of Bloomsbury. "Pozzo" was a nickname given to Maynard Keynes. The Hon. Dorothy Brett was the daughter of Lord Esher. An *habituée* of Garsington, she was a painter, and rather deaf. The future Lord Snowden was very crippled and of working-class origin.

"Massingberd" is a cruel joke on Massingham's name. Sir Archibald Armar Montgomery-Massingberd (1871–1947) was chief of staff to Lord Rawlinson in France from 1914 to 1918, and *his* position on the war was never in doubt.

Sir John Grenfell Maxwell (1859–1929) was commander-in-chief in Ireland in 1916. Lady Robert Cecil was the wife of the statesman who was an early and energetic supporter of the League of Nations. Admiral Sir Hedworth Meux (1856–1929) was formerly commander-in-chief at Portsmouth; at the time of writing he was a Conservative M.P. "Nathan" was Sir Matthew Nathan (1862–1939), undersecretary for Ireland from 1914 to 1916. He had been forced to resign his office, together with his chief, Augustine Birrell, owing to their alleged mishandling of the Easter Rebellion, which had taken place some weeks before this letter was written. Sir Matthew had once been a suitor of Strachey's sister Dorothy.

Mark Gertler (1891–1939) was the famous painter. His origins, as well as his physical beauty, probably struck Strachey as exotic. He was born in Spitalfields of Austro-Jewish parents.

Strachey wrote an essay on the occasion of the Prime Minister's visit to Garsington. It was published, with an introduction by Michael Holroyd, as "Asquith by Strachey" in *The Times*, 15 January 1972.

Garsington
May 31st 1916

Her Ladyship wants to know whether you would like to come down for the next week-end: Dickinson will be here. Or would you prefer the one after, which is Whitsuntide? Also, she hopes Noel could come too. Could you send a reply as soon as possible, as she seems a little distressed at nobody ever answering her invitations?

I hope poor Rose's books have been seen to. I had a most distressed letter from her. What had happened? From your pencil addition to her postcard, I had supposed that all was well.

The last week-end has been rather straining. Mr and Mrs Snowden, Mr Massingham, Bertie, Pozzo, to say nothing of Carrington and Brett. The Snowden couple were as provincial as one expected – she, poor woman, dreadfully plain and stiff, in stiff, plain clothes, and he with a strong northern accent, but also a certain tinge of eminence. Quite too political and remote from any habit of civilized discussion to make it possible to talk to him – one just had to listen to anecdotes and observations (good or bad); but a nice good-natured cripple. Lost Mr Massingberd came out much more than I'd foreshadowed – very much in the French style, and oh! so bitter. Talked a great deal about Ireland, where he's just been – says it's in the most fearful state – utter chaos and horror – and furious with the government. Apparently they knew Maxwell was a man of blood and iron, and must deliberately have chosen him for that purpose. The stories of the misconduct of the soldiery were very grim. As for Lloyd George's doing anything – quite out of the question. There was a most powerful anti-Cabinet atmosphere altogether; and then, as usual, in the middle of the Sunday afternoon torpor, the Prime Minister "and party" appeared. They *were* a scratch lot: – Lady Robert Cecil, stone deaf and smiling most sweetly at everything she didn't hear, a degraded Lady Meux (wife of Admiral Hedworth) with a paroqueet accent, and poor old Nathan, in walrus moustaches and an almost Uncle Trevor air of imbecile and louche benignity. I studied the Old Man with extreme vigour; and really he's a corker. He seemed much much larger than he did when I last saw him (just two years ago) – a fleshy, sanguine, wine-bibbing medieval-Abbot of a personage – a gluttonous, lecherous, cynical old fellow – oogh! – You should have seen him making towards Carrington – cutting her off at an angle as she crossed the lawn. I've rarely seen anyone so obviously enjoying life; so obviously, I thought, *out* to enjoy it; almost, really, as if he'd deliberately decided that he *would*, and let all the rest go hang. Cynical, yes, it's hardly possible to doubt it; or perhaps one should say just "case-hardened". *Tiens!* One looks at him, and thinks of the war. . . . And all the time, *perpetually*, a little, pointed, fat tongue comes poking out, and licking the great chops, and then darting back again. That gives one a sense of the Artful Dodger – the happy Artful Dodger – more even than the rest. His private boudoir doings with Ottoline are curious – if one's to believe what one hears; also his attitude towards Pozzo struck me – he positively sheered away from him. ("Not much juice in *him*," he said in private to her ladyship . . . so superficial, we all thought it!) Then why, oh why, does he go about with a creature like Lady Meux? On the whole, one wants to stick a dagger in his ribs . . . and then, as well, one can't help rather liking him – I suppose because he *does* enjoy himself so much. I felt most *sympathique* as I watched his conversation with Carrington.

Besides entertainments of this sort, I have been going through some other distractions. Rimbaud has been discovered, and (partly at any rate) read; which has led on to Verlaine, and re-reading and fresh reading of him – all very interesting; and their affair really absorbing. Then too I have been for some enormous walks – "expeditions" – with, precisely, Carrington. One was to the town of Abingdon, a magical spot, with a town-hall by Wren perhaps – a land of lotus-eaters, where I longed to sink down for the rest of my life, in an incredible oblivion . . . until I remembered that that's just what *has* been done, by . . . Lady Norman. As for Carrington, she's a queer young thing. These modern young women! What *are* they up to? They seem most highly dubious. Why is it? Is it because there's so much "in" them? Or so little? – They perplex me. When I consider Bunny, or Peter (he's close by, at Magdalen), or even Gertler, I find really nothing particularly obscure there, but when it comes to a creature with a cunt one seems to be immediately *désorienté*. Perhaps it's because cunts don't particularly appeal to me. I suppose that may be *partly* the explanation. But . . . oh, they coil, and coil; and, on the whole, they make me uneasy.

What is happening to you? Il Gran' Pozzo told me you had settled into an office for the succouring of our German inmates. So I presume that all is well. I gathered also from handwriting on forwarded envelopes that Pernel was at Belsize. I fear London must be horribly stuffy. My health is I think better – but not very much. I don't yet feel what I consider I ought to. And I'm still liable to those attacks (though only faintly). I've hardly an idea how long I shall stay. My hopes for the more distant future are pinned to the fruitfarm.

The C.O. question seems to be hanging fire. Everyone declares that as soon as this bill is safely over, "something" will be done. In the meantime, nothing absolutely nothing, is. The P.M. promised Pipsey, Bertie, Snowden, etc., with his own mouth that the detachment in France should be brought back; not only has this not been done, but more have been sent there. But what can you expect from a 20th century Silenus?

Do send a postcard or something in re coming here. And Noel? –

Rimbaud, I assure you, is a good poet.

Yours

Lytton

This letter deals with the infamous proceedings against Bertrand Russell. In April a conscientious objector called Ernest F. Everett who was a member of the N.C.F. had been sentenced to two years' hard labour for defiance of military orders. On 19 April the N.C.F. published a leaflet protesting the sentence, and six of its members were arrested and imprisoned for distributing it. In a letter to *The Times* Russell acknowledged authorship of the leaflet, and insisted that if anyone should be prosecuted it ought to be himself. The authorities immediately instituted proceedings against Russell, and on 5 June 1916 he appeared at the Mansion House before the Lord Mayor, Sir Charles Wakefield, and was charged with publishing "statements likely to prejudice the recruiting discipline of His Majesty's forces". A. H. Bodkin (1862–1957), later Sir Archibald Bodkin, Director of Public Prosecutions between 1920 and 1930, appeared for the prosecution. Russell conducted his own defence. The presence of Lytton Strachey, together with Lady Ottoline Morrell, who was strikingly apparelled, rather enhanced the proceedings.

[6 June 1916]
Monday

Verdict – Fine of £100. Defendant appealed. B.R. spoke for about an hour – quite well – but simply a propaganda speech. The Lord Mayor looked like a stuck pig. Counsel for the prosecution was an incredible Daumier caricature of a creature – and positively turned out to be Mr Bodkin. I felt rather nervous in that Brigands' cave.

G.L.S.

I don't like the type of letter from me you select to leave about.

Eva Gore-Booth, sister of Countess Markievicz and fond of riding to hounds, so impressed Yeats with her beauty that he wrote a poem celebrating it. She had poetic ambitions herself, but spent her life in aiding rather woolly political causes.

Evan Morgan, later Viscount Tredegar (1899–1949), was at the time an undergraduate at Christ Church.

"Arnold" refers to Strachey's essay on Dr Arnold which became part of *Eminent Victorians*.

Strachey's companion at Wells was Dora Carrington.

James Strachey's companion in Scotland was his future wife, Alix Sargant-Florence. The Stracheys were closely related to the Grants of Rothiemurchus, "the Family" referred to by James.

Julian Grenfell (1888–1915) was a poet, killed in action as was his brother William (1890–1915). Their father was W. H. Grenfell, afterwards Lord Desborough. Julian Grenfell's celebrated poem "Into Battle" appeared in *The Times* on the day his death was announced. Bertrand Russell's lectures referred to in the fourth letter below were published as *Principles of Social Reconstruction*.

Garsington Manor
Oxford
July 15th 1916

I am sending the key in another envelope. Yesterday I received from the War Office Form W.3299, notifying that in accordance with sub-section 2 of section 3 of the Military Service Act (Session 2) I am required to present myself again for medical inspection before September 30th. The Form is headed "Notice Paper to be sent to a man who offered himself for enlistment and was rejected since August 14th 1915". Philip's notion is that it does not apply to me, and certainly (on my view) I did *not* offer myself for enlistment, but claimed exemption from the local tribunal and got it. He advises me to write to Lt Parkinson to this effect, and to suggest that he has made a mistake. What do you think? Is it possible that the new Act subjects everyone rejected for health by the Tribunals to re-examination? Have you got a copy of the bloody thing? Of course Pipsey hasn't. It would be awful to have to go through all that again – with the possibility of clerkism or prison at the end of it.

It has been and still is extremely whirlpoolish here. The house is crammed and this afternoon 5 more people enter it. Last weekend Clifford Allen came – I thought a dismal figure. So painfully lower-middle-class. What hope is there in that sort of thing? Eva Gore-Booth was really better.

Now there is Evan Morgan (an aristocratic abortion) sleeping with me in the cottage – for I've been relegated there. He's half witted, unfortunately, with a paroqueet nose, so, beyond reading his poems ("Death's ramage" rhyming to "scrimage" (sic)), I don't make much progress. On the whole I hardly think I'm long for this region, and shall probably melt in about a week to Durbins. But will that be any better? I wrote to Hern to try to get Becky for September, but it's full up. *Où aller donc?*

The weather is very heavy and repulsive. I've begun to write Arnold, but it's an arduous affair. Is there any news?

Yr

Lytton

36

The Swan Hotel,
Wells,
Somerset.
Aug. 28th 1916

I have just found your letter here. I wonder where you are –
where, oh where? I can guarantee that the North is fatal, as I've
just come from it – nothing but rain and icy winds. I caught a
chill on the top of a mountain, and have not yet recovered, damn
it. Unfortunately, however, the South seems as bad: it is pouring
here, and so cold that I've been obliged to buy woollen mufflers
and fur-lined gloves. I don't know in the least where I shall go or
what will become of me. Couldn't we join somehow or somewhere? Perhaps if you addressed a letter to this place, it would
eventually reach me. *Quelle misère!* And the "Cathedral" is so
ugly. . . . My Quantock lodging is off – too expensive – perhaps
Bridgwater. But money? . . . Have *you* got any? Or are you staying with friends?

My companion leaves me tomorrow, I fancy, so then I shall be
quite alone. One word, I beg.

Yours

Lytton

c/o Mr John MacKenzie
Upper Tullochgrue
Rothiemurchus
September 8th 1916

I'm sorry to have drifted off. Your account of the North is absurd.
I left London in a blizzard of fog and sleet, and found it simply
tropical here. The sun beats down, the sweat pours from the face –
we can't even bear a fire in the evening. This is perhaps the best of
all positions – the rooms face the mountains, and one's quite a
mile further into the forest than usual. It's also a thousand feet
high; and the cooking etc. are replete with excellence.

The Sheriff was at Aviemore to meet us; but seemed rather
upset by "my", as you'ld say, "companion". I don't think we'll be
bothered by the Family.

37

I suppose you won't change your mind and come up here? Bob Trevy is expected shortly.

> *Yours faithfully,*
>
> *J.S.*

> *The Manor House*
> *Garsington*
> *Oxford*
> *Nov. 27th 1916*

I shall return on Wednesday. It is very fine and fresh here, but damned cold. So far most of my diseases have increased, but I hope this is only the result of the first plunge, and that the reaction will shortly set in.

The Massing Bird and Maynard have been the chief figurants for the week-end. The former kept up his usual *tout est perdu* strain, which is on the whole rather comforting. He says that the wheat supply will probably break down, that nobody in high quarters knows in the least what to do in any circumstances, and that the army is on the point of mutiny. He made a long speech (to Maynard and me in the cab from the station) on the condition of the barracks – filth, vermin, bullying, murders of sergeants, venereal disease rampant, and "finally – sodomy". He seems decidedly perturbed. His only satisfaction is in the fact that L.G. is as much loathed by the War Office as by all the other persons he's come in contact with. The ex-Butler had dinner with Haldane the other day, and spent the whole time in a tirade of complaints. He wound up with "there's only one word for it, Lord 'Aldane, it's bloody piss".

Maynard, of course, preserves his official optimism. He thinks the war will end before long – that is to say before next October. He also thinks that we shall manage the wheat supply, though he admits that sugar has altogether gone. He thinks that Doc W. will intervene in the Spring, and that we shall bow to his instructions. Well, well! *I* shouldn't be at all surprised if there was some ghastly catastrophe the day after tomorrow, – and then we should find the Sybilline Books applied in a way not at all to the taste of the

Spectator. And, by God, I shouldn't after that much care to be in the skin of a politician.

Mr and Mrs Shove and Clive are in the cottage opposite, and seem very cheerful, so far. Besides the war, conversation has run almost entirely on the Grenfell Dioscuri – and it appeared that both her Ladyship and Pozzo were secretly in love with them. All agreed that every effort must be made to get the book published at once.

I have gone through Bertie's lectures again, and find them most exhilarating. If they come from Bickers, you'd better open the parcel.

The Times today seems to be fairly shaking in its shoes about South Wales. Mr M. thought that the article with extracts from *The New York Times* on peace *was tendencieux*.

Yours

Lytton

COMMENTARY
"SENNACHERIB AND RUPERT BROOKE"

Sennacherib was king of Assyria from 705 to 681 B.C. He spent most of his reign fighting to maintain the empire founded by his father. He waged a bloody campaign in 701 against an uprising of the western nations, Phoenicia, Palestine and Philistia, who were supported by Egypt, and threatened Jerusalem itself. Byron's poem, "The Destruction of Sennacherib", relies on the Biblical account in II Chronicles 32.

Rupert Brooke died in the Aegean in 1915 at the age of twenty-seven of blood-poisoning. He was an early friend of Strachey's, and Strachey's brother James was infatuated with Brooke, whose good looks were legendary. Brooke mistakenly blamed Lytton Strachey for the rupture of his affair with Ka Cox, and, as an ardent soldier himself, turned against his former friends who had become conscientious objectors. It is possible to read a reference to the Strachey brothers and others of their circle into the lines from the first war sonnet:

> Leave the sick hearts that honour could not move,
> And half-men, and their dirty songs and dreary . . .

For his part, Strachey disliked intensely Brooke's attitude to the war, but was very moved by the report of Brooke's death.

The genre Strachey employs here is an unusual one, the dialogue of the dead. A form of classical origin, it found much favour with eighteenth-century French and English writers, but Strachey was perhaps the only English writer to employ it since then. He seems to have made a careful study of the conventions governing the form, for the ten dialogues he composed all have the ghosts of historical characters conversing in the classical underworld, are written in prose, and have no preceding narrative to set the scene or to expound the circumstances of the conversation. Like most practitioners of this form, Strachey uses it for satirical ends. In this brief and carefully polished example, Strachey brings out the similarity of Rupert Brooke's position on war to Sennacherib's, thus under-cutting Brooke's position by showing it to be quite as nasty as that of the bloodthirsty barbarian. None of the dialogues bears a date, and it may be that they were undertaken as exercises in literary discipline.

At St Paul's on Easter Sunday, 1915, Dean Inge preached a sermon that incorporated Brooke's sonnet "The Soldier", which begins with the famous lines

> If I should die think only this of me:
>   That there's some corner of a foreign field
> That is for ever England . . .

Brooke received a report of the proceedings at the cathedral a short time before his death.

SENNACHERIB AND RUPERT BROOKE

SENNACHERIB. Another war, I hear. Quite so. Excellent.

RUPERT BROOKE. Another? Impossible.

SENNACHERIB. Always another. That is the beauty of it. Human nature is so cleverly constructed that one war gives birth to the next, in an endless series. It never stops. There are a few intervals, of course, just long enough for a breathing-space and the necessary preparations, and then we are at it again. The world is a wonderful place.

RUPERT BROOKE. And yet it would be more wonderful still if there were no wars.

SENNACHERIB. What? What is that? Are you a pacifist?

RUPERT BROOKE. Not at all. I am a soldier. I think that a war, if it is for some good cause, may be not only justifiable, but admirable; I think that then it is every man's duty to take part in it, and that the noblest of occupations is to fight.

SENNACHERIB. Quite so. Excellent. And what was the cause you fought for?

RUPERT BROOKE. In the first place, I fought for England.

SENNACHERIB. England? What is that? I have never heard of it. Is it your God? My God is Nisrock – a very fine God, let me tell you, with a hawk's head, a man's legs, and a lion's talons.

RUPERT BROOKE. England is my country.

SENNACHERIB. Your country! Quite so. Excellent. There is nothing more serviceable than patriotism.

RUPERT BROOKE. My friends and I were convinced that England stood for honour and liberty; and so we went to take the Dardanelles, in obedience to the instructions of Mr Winston Churchill.

SENNACHERIB. Honour! Liberty! Quite so. Excellent. Now tell me this: I believe you write poetry; am I right?

RUPERT BROOKE. I have written some poetry.

SENNACHERIB. Better and better! Just the sort of young fellow I should have wished for in my own army. Not that my army lacked poets, either. I remember one young man who wrote some very remarkable verses, to the effect that if he happened to be killed on foreign service, wherever he might be buried, there would be a piece of Assyria. Most striking. The High Priest of Nineveh preached a sermon on it in the temple of Nisrock, and everyone was deeply impressed.

RUPERT BROOKE. But they had no right to be. Assyria did not stand for honour and liberty; she stood for power and wickedness; her war with Egypt was a mere struggle for domination; and if I had lived under your rule, I should have been a conscientious objector.

SENNACHERIB. Tut, tut, tut! You are quite mistaken. You know nothing of the facts. Our war with Egypt was undertaken purely for self-defence; it was also undertaken to preserve the rights of the smaller nationalities. Egypt was aiming at a world-empire. Every right-thinking person in Assyria would have told you that. It was a necessary war, a just war, and a glorious war. The slaughter was enormous, and the devastation greater than had ever been known. And we defeated Egypt. Nothing could have been more entirely admirable from every point of view.

RUPERT BROOKE. But when you had won, how did you use your victory? Surely that is the crucial question.

SENNACHERIB. I don't follow you. I was talking about the war, and you ask me about the peace. When peace came, I grant you, it was less satisfactory; to my mind, it always is. We promised the Egyptians that if they yielded we would not despoil them beyond a certain point; they yielded; and then we decided to despoil them utterly. At the same time, having starved them while the war was proceeding, we continued to starve them after it was over. Then the Arabians had a revolution, and we starved them. We deprived the Abyssinians of all their fruitful territory, and we forbade them to trade, so they starved too. Altogether it was a very difficult situation; but we did our best. We got up subscriptions for the poor starving Arabians and Abyssinians, and sent them several loaves of bread. Quite so. Excellent. And yet, somehow or other, the world continued to be restless, and people complained; until at last I am happy to say the atmosphere was cleared in a highly satisfactory manner – there was another inevitable war.

RUPERT BROOKE. So that is your record! Then I can only say that our war had no resemblance whatever to yours.

SENNACHERIB. Young man, I beg leave to doubt it. I have had a long experience of wars, and in my judgement there is never a pin to choose between them. But I see what you mean; you mean that your war was more thorough than mine; and there perhaps you are right. Though I could do things on a big scale, too. I remember once I sent an army of 180,000 men into Palestine, where it was destroyed with quite extraordinary suddenness by some microbe or other. As the native chronicler put it, when they arose early in the morning, behold, they were all dead corpses. Quite so. Excellent. But I admit that such dramatic casualty lists were rare in my days; and I envy you your guns, your submarines, your aeroplanes, and your gas.

RUPERT BROOKE. You are a barbarian and a tyrant, and you misunderstand me completely. Every word that you utter fills me with disgust. But let me tell you once again that the war I fought in was like none that you were ever concerned with. It was noble, generous, high-intentioned. It was a war to bring peace and justice into the world. And how can I doubt that it has done so? What is passing on earth is hidden from me; but how could I dream for a moment that England should fail?

SENNACHERIB. That is the spirit! Quite so. Excellent. I shall always be perfectly contented so long as there are soldiers such as you.

COMMENTARY
"LORD PETTIGREW"

Lord Pettigrew was intended to be a political novel, but Strachey only completed the first draft of the first four chapters before abandoning the project; parts of chapters I, II and IV appear here. It is of interest not only because it shows Strachey trying his hand at a novel, but also because it allows us a glimpse of the evolution of Strachey's political views. As an undergraduate, Keynes remarked of Strachey, politics was only "a fairly adequate substitute for bridge". From internal evidence the date of the composition of *Lord Pettigrew* can be set between 1908 and 1911, and the work was obviously intended as a commentary on nearly contemporary events, for the novel is set in 1909. An outline pencilled on the back of the last sheet of the manuscript makes it possible to reconstruct, if not the plot, than at least the themes of the novel.

Some of the topics Strachey intended to deal with in the work were socialism, the Lloyd George Budget, tariff reform, the navy, conscription, reform of the House of Lords, India, the Poor Law, old age pensions, women's suffrage, divorce, the family, and censorship. Several of these are touched on in the first four chapters. Strachey also lists his characters, and the settings for the episodes of the novel. Most of the characters were to be aristocrats, and the settings were, appropriately, various locations in a stately home and the village to which it was attached. This is important, not only because Strachey had a closer acquaintance with the running of a ducal household than with the running of a socialist political meeting; but also because Strachey's method was to have the upper classes appear as the villains of his novel by condemning themselves out of their own mouths. This method can be illustrated by the conversation in Chapter II between Lord Pettigrew, Lord Valerian, and Lord Castle Mainwaring, in which the dialogue makes it clear that it is not Lloyd George or Keir Hardie who are the real enemies of parliamentary democracy, but these reactionary noblemen and their fellows in the House of Lords.

The choice of issues to be dealt with in the novel and the handling of them in the chapters he completed show a progress on Strachey's part from undergratuate apathy to keen political interest. Far from having become interested in politics only when he was personally threatened with conscription in 1916, he was already an advanced Liberal by 1909–11, when he wrote this fragment of *Lord Pettigrew*. It is difficult to discern whether Strachey disliked the aristocracy as a whole, or only its reactionary and philistine aspects; certainly, after his literary success in the twenties he did not object to being lionized by society hostesses.

The plan of *Lord Pettigrew* is frankly didactic; for the most part, the extant chapters are more interesting for the issues they deal with than for the quality of the writing. An exception is the passage in Chapter IV in which Lady Valerian takes Lady Phyllis Belton on a tour of Sloanes, the stately home in which most of the novel is set. Strachey is so sensitive to the feeling of history that one experiences in such houses, and to the beauty of their architecture, that his writing rises well above the heavily ironical style of the early chapters. He is also rather good on the character of the arch-philistine Lady Valerian. Close observation of the intricacies of individual personalities was, after all, one of Strachey's great talents, as his published works show, and he might have succeeded as a novelist if he had continued along the lines indicated by Chapter IV. If one excepts the purely topical references to the Lloyd George budget and similar issues, many of the concerns of the proposed novel seem curiously timely and modern, in spite of the fact that they are the sort of concerns reflected in all comedies of manners. For example, in Chapter III (which is not included in this selection), characters are made to comment on the strange dress affected by the younger generation, and to ridicule its taste in art. The conversation that makes up most of Chapter II is included here for its reflection of Strachey's interest in politics, rather than for its merit as imaginative literature. With its exact rendering of the language of the Upper House, and its long and complicated speeches, it can perhaps be seen as a twentieth-century attempt at euphuism, having all the irony of that Renaissance style, but little of its wit. It might also be remarked by the reader that Strachey is much more successful in the portrayal of his female characters than of his male ones, and that the long disquisition on Lady Valerian shows a very modern sensibility when he touches on the question of the social roles of women – even when the woman in question aspires to become a duchess.

In this selection three dots in the text indicate material omitted by the editor.

LORD PETTIGREW

§

CHAPTER I

It was half past three when Viscount Pettigrew arrived at the station, and decided, as the day was so agreeable, to walk across the park. Leaving his man to take the luggage in the motor, he stepped briskly across the road – for the way was familiar to him – and passed through a wicket-gate on the other side. The park undulated before him, green and glorious in the September sunlight, the great beeches scattering themselves majestically along the slopes of grass and bracken, and the distant prospect all a haze. Lord Pettigrew was dressed with absolute propriety; his hat (a felt one, divided in the middle), his dark clothes, neither old nor new, and the perfection of his boots – these things revealed at once the distinguished English gentleman. His face and figure, small, well-proportioned, middle-aged, seemed accustomed – one could not quite tell why – to consideration and authority. Unfortunately, however, Lord Pettigrew squinted; and this produced in his appearance an impression of uneasiness and uncertainty, which it was difficult to get over. As he walked along the footpath, he felt, as indeed he often did, slightly annoyed. The sight of the park brought instinctively into his mind his own parks, in Dorsetshire, in Yorkshire, and in Ireland, with their respective advantages. He thought of the long avenue at Melworth, the fishponds at Rackham Abbey, and the white cattle at Ballygloe; and then, just for a moment, there occurred to him the possibility of something

47

happening, and his losing them. Something – his imagination went no further; he was almost frightened by its going so far as that; but his rising annoyance left him no room for anything else. . . . His surroundings had grown faintly dissatisfying. The landscape, the air, the walk, the whole temper of things, seemed somehow not altogether as they should be. He continued on his path with his accustomed assurance; but, in the background of his consciousness, there still lurked an unpleasant something, an uncomfortable, a vexing, an almost menacing presence, which Lord Pettigrew could not understand.

All at once a polite young man stepped out from a clump of beeches, and advanced towards him.

"Excuse me. Lord Pettigrew?" said the polite young man.

"I am Lord Pettigrew," replied the nobleman.

"Lady Valerian thought you might walk," said the young man. "She asked me to wait for you. I'm Lord Valerian's secretary."

"I'm delighted to meet you," said Lord Pettigrew, with courtesy, offering his hand. "Will you walk with me, Mr –?"

"Oh, Baker," said the young man, quickly shaking hands. Then, as they walked along together, "It was about the Duke," he explained, "that Lady Valerian asked me to speak to you."

Lord Pettigrew was immediately grave. "The Duke! Nothing – I hope –"

"Oh no; his Grace is perfectly well; his health is excellent. It's nothing physical that's the matter. It's only" – Mr Baker paused; "it's only the memory."

"The memory?" echoed Lord Pettigrew.

"Yes," continued Mr Baker, "there seems to be an unfortunate lapse in the memory – especially, if I may say so, the political memory. For a man with, as you know, Lord Pettigrew, his Grace's remarkable interest in politics" – Lord Pettigrew nodded – "it's all the more extraordinary – painful even – that this should have occurred. So far as we can find out, the Duke has no recollection whatever of anything subsequent to 1906 – the General Election of 1906. He appears to have forgotten what happened then, and what has happened ever since. It's as if there was a blank in his mind."

Lord Pettigrew was startled. "But in that case, how does he get over the present situation?"

"He does not get over it," replied Mr Baker. "He ignores it.

He believes, Lord Pettigrew, that the Unionists are still in power."

"Dear me!" said Lord Pettigrew, "this is most singular; the Duke, of course, is an old man" –

"He will be eighty-three in January," said Mr Baker.

– "Eighty-three in January; exactly. But that does not account for such a strange hallucination. The Unionists still in power! Most painful! Have no efforts been made, Mr Baker, to disabuse him?"

"Every effort has been made, but without effect. It was never easy, as you know, Lord Pettigrew, to make an impression on his Grace" – Lord Pettigrew nodded – "and now it seems impossible. References to the Government or the Budget or things of that kind he simply brushes aside. He won't have it. The situation's difficult. He pays no attention to hints, and how can one say straight out that he's forgotten what's known to everyone? One morning at breakfast young Mr Roderick did, but it made things no better. 'My dear boy,' said the Duke, 'you're arguing as if Lloyd George were Chancellor of the Exchequer.' – 'But, Grandpapa, he *is*,' replied Mr Roderick."

"Dear, dear!" ejaculated Lord Pettigrew. "And what happened then?"

"Everyone looked at their plates," replied Mr Baker. "It was a very awkward moment; but, curiously enough, the one person who wasn't embarrassed was his Grace. He was only very angry, asked Mr Roderick what he meant, told him that it was very wrong to say such things as that even in joke, and dismissed him from the breakfast table. Lady Valerian was afraid that Mr Roderick would try to argue it out, and he was actually beginning to, when his father ordered him most severely to leave the room."

"Quite right, in my opinion," said Lord Pettigrew.

"For the rest of the day," continued Mr Baker, "the Duke was upset and irritable, and he hardly slept at night. The result was that Lord Valerian requested everybody in future to refer as little as possible to current politics while the Duke was present, and, if they were obliged to, to accept his Grace's view. That seemed both to him and to Lady Valerian the best course to follow; so far it has been successful, though it is not always easy, as you can imagine, Lord Pettigrew, to carry it out."

Lord Pettigrew nodded. "And it was this that you came to tell me?"

"To ask you," said Mr Baker, "to fall in as much as possible with his Grace. That was Lady Valerian's message."

"I'm very much obliged, very much obliged indeed," said Lord Pettigrew. "I shall, of course, be most careful. To my mind, a highly proper precaution."

"There was also," said Mr Baker, producing a letter, "this from Lady Castle Mainwaring."

"Lady Castle Mainwaring," said Lord Pettigrew, taking it. "Is she here?"

"She and Lord Castle Mainwaring have come over for a few days from Cumber."

"Ah!" said Lord Pettigrew. "Perhaps, Mr Baker, you will precede me? Tell Lady Valerian, please, that I shall be discretion itself."

When the secretary's broad back had disappeared down a grove of chestnuts, Lord Pettigrew opened the small scented envelope, and read as follows:

Dearest darling Doloo

Was it cross then, was it? Did it go away from its *own* little Moggie on the terrace without so much as a good night? Oh naughty, naughty! So just *one little* letter before it sees its Moggie to say that Moggie's oh *so* frightened and would like to know that her darling Doloo isn't cross still – and will Doloo make its handkerchief hang out of its *dear* pocket so that she may know if it's not when we meet? *Dear* Sammy is taking this, who's *discretion itself*, so good-bye now darling your Moggs.

Lord Pettigrew disposed the letter in an inner pocket. "Dear Mary's so romantic," he muttered to himself, almost smiling, as he arranged his handkerchief.

CHAPTER II

"Lend me thy handkerchief" – *Othello*

The next moment two stalwart forms appeared upon the path, and Lord Pettigrew recognized Lord Valerian and Lord Castle

Mainwaring. He was by no means pleased. He would have been very glad to have a few words with Lord Valerian alone; but the presence of Lord Castle Mainwaring, he knew from long experience, never failed to be disturbing; what else could be expected from a man who always talked too much? The Marquis of Valerian was as large and as handsome as befitted the heir to the dukedom of Cheshire; and he came forward with that demeanour of amiable solidity which he never lacked. The Earl of Castle Mainwaring was less imposing; though his area was almost as immense, it was without the perfect absence of emphasis which brought his companion's appearance to the verge of the superhuman; his figure was corpulent, his face was excited and full of blood, and his eyes projected from under their thick black brows in a way that was not encouraging.

"Well, what's the news?" he said, when the salutations were over.

Lord Pettigrew did not like questions. "The situation is somewhat difficult," was his reply. But an answer was the last thing that the Earl had wanted. "In my opinion," he went on, almost without a pause, "the next thing we shall hear is that they've dropped it – dropped the whole blasted thing. They've been at it now for four months, and they can't go on for ever. Lloyd George is weak – a coward at bottom – Birmingham showed that plain enough – to run away in a policeman's helmet after his dastardly abuse of our men – I've a good mind to write to *The Times* about it – it's a thing people shouldn't forget. The insolence of a man like that –! But it can't go on much longer; the thing's impossible. All the respectable liberals – the moderate men – are sick of him – sick as they can be. Only yesterday Sir Roper Rampton told me he'd voted for them for the last thirty years – except once at the Home Rule election – and that this was more than he could stand. 'A man must draw the line somewhere,' he said, 'and I draw it at Lloyd George.' I told him that that was what half the Cabinet would say, if they said what they thought. How they can –! Good heavens! To be led by the nose by a Welsh attorney! Is it worth it? I ask you, is it worth it, at five thousand a year? Never mind, he's got himself tied up in such a mess in the House of Commons, he'll go pip one of these days – chuck it all up – perform the happy despatch; his last chance, I should say, for saving himself with the country."

"The country," said Lord Pettigrew; "the country is an elusive entity."

"If they drop the budget," said Lord Valerian, "what will become of the services?"

"What ever happens," said Lord Castle Mainwaring, "they only have themselves to thank. It's they who've made the blessed muddle, and it's their business to get out of it as best they can. Anyone can see that. The only question is whether they will ever get out of it. One thing's clear and that is that the budget will have to go sooner or later; if they don't drop it in the Commons, do you think, my dear Valerian, that we'll stick it in the Lords?"

Lord Pettigrew had been waiting for this; and, though he was a little disconcerted when the question was addressed not to him, but to Lord Valerian –, who, after all, was not a peer – he was ready with his exposition. "The question is a complex one," he began; but Lord Castle Mainwaring was not to be interrupted.

"The whole business," continued that excited nobleman, "is as plain as a pike-staff. What are the Lords for, if they're not to control the Commons? You may do away with us, if you like; you may have a single-chamber government – to my mind a monstrosity and a delusion, and a thing, mark you, unknown in any civilized country on the face of the globe; you may do that, but if you don't – and nobody proposes that you should except Mr Keir Hardie – then you must lump us, and have done with it. Is it logical, I ask you, is it logical to have a system such as ours, a – a –" Lord Castle Mainwaring hesitated – "a what you may call it –"

"A bi-cameral system," put in Lord Pettigrew.

"Exactly, a bi-cameral system, in which one of the chambers can do nothing but what the other wants? Why, it's self-contradictory on the face of it. And then they bother us with what they're pleased to call the Constitution. Who cares twopence-halfpenny for the Constitution, I should like to know, – for a resolution passed two hundred years ago by heaven knows who? Who *can* care for such things except professors and dons and people who write long letters to the *Spectator*? The thing's absurd. Our business is perfectly clear – it's simply to do our duty, to do what we consider best for the country, whatever your precious House of Commons may think, and whatever the question may be – finance or seats for shop girls, it's all the same. In this case, the welfare of the nation depends on our sending to the right about a crew of piratical tatterdemalions who've managed, somehow or other, to get control of the Government. Anyone can see what they're up to. They're simply trying, with their blessed budget, to strike at the landed interest – at us, in fact, – at the very people whose existence is a bar to the dominion of demagogues. These taxes are vindictive and predatory to the last degree." Lord Castle Mainwaring, as he warmed, gradually assumed his platform manner. – "They talk of the re-adjustment of wealth by means of taxation – a most dangerous doctrine, if I may say so with great respect, without a very careful examination of what it means. Gentlemen, you will have a re-adjustment of wealth by means of taxation, if you legalize pickpockets. Is that the object that is set before us? I believe it comes very near being the object of the present government. The super tax is an interference with the liberty of the subject; the land-tax is a direct attack on capital. Admit the principle, my lords, once admit the principle, and what is the distinction between a halfpenny in the pound and five shillings or ten shillings in the pound? It is impossible to draw a line; by one turn of the screw, some young man at five hundred a year will mulct you of whatever you please. Let me take the case of a man of fifty who owns a million. What is his position? Suppose he has the very earnest and proper desire to leave his property, which he received from his father, to his son, without any reduction. What must he do? Under this budget he must insure to the tune of nine thousand a year. Nine thousand a year, gentlemen, with a capital of a million! And not only he, but his son, his grandson, and his great grandson must pay nine thousand a year for all time to keep the estate intact. If the head of the family happens to have more than one son – if that happens – then God knows what he will do – I leave it to your lordships' imagination. We shall very soon be told that when a man comes into a fortune by his energy or his good luck that the Chancellor of the Exchequer has the right to step in, declare the wealth is the result of swindling or blackmailing, and take a share of the plunder. And for what? For old-age pensions, perhaps? Oh, so he says; but it's in reality to finance this or that scheme of some socialist body which must be placated to keep the Government in office. Everyone knows that these people are simply socialists. The Prime Minister himself the other day positively maintained that there were certain sums of money which would be better employed if they were taken from the individual for the good of the State. If that's not socialism, I really don't know what is. It's our plain duty – the duty of the Upper House – to protect the country from being bullied, jockeyed, and bluffed by two irresponsible mountebanks into a budget and a policy for which I make bold to say there was not the slightest mandate at the last General Election. The House of Lords represents every moderate man in the country, it represents the working classes, it represents the nation itself." – Lord Castle Mainwaring drew a breath for his peroration – "Its relations with the Lower House are in themselves a monument, if I may say so, a monument to the sagacity of the English people. For centuries the delicate and subtle equipoise has been preserved unchanged, substantially unchanged, by the statecraft of great politicians, so that today it bears something of that mysterious sanctity which can be given by Time and by nothing else. And now this magnificent fabric – a fabric which has won – I say it without fear of contradiction – the admiration of the civilized world, this amazing monument and this unique expression of the temperament of our race is to be shattered – shattered, gentlemen, shattered and destroyed – at the bidding of a demagogue from Wales!"

Just as Lord Castle Mainwaring uttered these words, the path, which had been winding slowly up a gradual incline, took a sudden turn, and the three friends found themselves upon a small plateau commanding an extended view of the surrounding country. On the horizon, beyond wide stretches of pasturage and verdure, the church tower of the county of Misseter could be discerned; and close below, in the middle distance, there lay, among its gardens, its waters, and its elm-trees, the great house of Sloanes. A rustic bench, conveniently placed under a clump of beeches, allured the walkers, who automatically sat down. Lord Castle Mainwaring was not sorry for the rest; he was too corpulent a man to be able, with any comfort, to deliver a speech on an up-hill walk in the warmth of a September afternoon. He was not only out of breath, but unpleasantly hot and perspiring. "Pooh!" he exclaimed, as he sat down, "I'm swimming in sweat"; and he took off his hat to mop his forehead. He was annoyed, however, to find that he had forgotten his handkerchief – it was in none of his pockets. He was on the point of an oath, when his eye caught a large white expanse of inviting cambric, dangling almost under his nose from Lord Pettigrew's coat. It was too much to resist. "Oh, Pettigrew, lend me this," he genially gasped. "I've lost my own," and, without waiting for an answer, seized the handkerchief and applied it, before his companion could prevent him, to the required purpose.

Lord Pettigrew was so angry that for a moment he was deprived of speech. His irritation had been steadily growing during Lord Castle Mainwaring's oration; he had been interrupted, ignored, and obliged to listen to a flood of observations which were all the more annoying from there being nothing in them to which he did not agree. In substance, they represented his own sentiments with an almost painful accuracy; the arguments were excellent arguments; and some of the points even – the young man with five hundred a year was one – he remembered with a pang had originated with himself. No, it was not the substance, it was the form, of Lord Castle Mainwaring's remarks that was distressing. The method of expression was ill-advised, the whole tone overstrained, injudicious, and unconciliatory. If even he had been nearly pushed into antagonism, what would be the feelings of a professed opponent or, worse still, of a moderate man? The seizure of his handkerchief was the last straw. Was the man deliberately attempting to make him ridiculous? How on earth would he explain to Mary? It was really too much. For a moment he was silent, and then he determined to assert himself and to speak.

"The question is a complex one," he repeated with severity. "It is one which cannot be decided by an appeal, however forcible and coloured, to first principles or to logic – after all what is logic? – it is a question of policy and fact. You are doubtless in possession of channels of information which are denied to me; but I have yet to learn with any certitude that a reference to the ballot would substantially alleviate the condition of affairs. In many quarters the contrary is anticipated – with what justice I shall not pretend to determine. But at least it is clear that there may be many reasons for postponing a final and momentous decision to a possibly more favourable juncture, and from refraining from an action, which, whatever its theoretical justification, may, in fact, merely precipitate disaster."

The official style of these words, and the authoritative manner in which Lord Pettigrew uttered them, produced the effect which he had hoped for. On each side of him, his bully companions sat silent. "After all," he thought, "I am one of their leaders; I have a right to speak." Lord Castle Mainwaring was still mopping his brow. At last Lord Valerian made an observation. "I understand," he said. "If the budget is thrown out, there will be a general election." Upon that, Lord Castle Mainwaring opened his mouth, and Lord Pettigrew, foreseeing another outburst, and detecting, with the certainty of long habit, the signs of Tariff Reform and Unemployment in his neighbour's eye, decided that it was time to turn the conversation.

"This is a delightful prospect, Valerian," he quickly said. "We are placed high."

"Yes," replied Lord Valerian, with his imperturbable suavity. "It's a very pleasant spot; and high – decidedly. The ground falls away on every side." ...

CHAPTER IV

Lady Valerian was a tall, angular woman of almost fifty. She would have been considered handsome, for her features were large and regular, if her appearance had not so absolutely lacked the elements of grace. As one looked at her, it was impossible to believe that she had ever attracted anyone, or – is it only another way of putting it? – that she had ever been attracted. And her looks did not belie her. She had come through life, in the midst of wealth, honour and consideration, without the faintest experience of any of those feelings which lend a beauty and an elevation to existence – without affection, without passion, without effort, without success, without happiness, and without hope. None the less she was, in the common acceptation of the term, a good woman; that is to say she was not vicious. Indeed, she was as far removed from vice as she was from taste, knowledge, and intelligence; and she performed her duties under the same inborn impulsion that made her dislike music and never open a book. Thus, though she seemed to move in virtue, the reward of it perpetually escaped her. She was one of those people who are certain to go into eternal bliss, and who are equally certain, even there, not to enjoy themselves. Disappointment was her natural element – she had a talent for it, one might almost have said – but it was a disappointment of the negative kind; not the fierce agony of baffled desire, but the dull empty unfulfilment of an unimagined Might-have-been. She had always lived in the country, and she had always been bored. Her youth had been spent in the drudgery of keeping house in a great establishment, for her mother had died young, and Lord Northingbury, old, proud, foolish, and popular, had lived for nothing but county hospitality and the feudal glories of Crowborough Castle. She took no pleasure in preparing for entertainments which she disliked, and in being polite to neighbours whom she despised; but she gave up her existence to these things with so religious a propriety that even the pleasures of dissatisfaction were denied to her. Her one solace had been the hunting-field, and there alone, in the grim exhilaration of a cross-country gallop, she had sometimes forgotten that she was Lady Gertrude Galt. Unfortunately, on one occasion she stayed out with the hounds so long that when she returned the carriages of the guests for a magnificent dinner-party were rolling through the gates of the Castle. She reached her room unobserved, by a side entrance; but her father was the pink of punctuality, and she felt that nothing in the world could be worse than to be late. She had time to perform the shortest of toilets, to put on her pearls, and to exchange her habit for a dress – she could do no more, and as it was, when she came into the drawing-room, the company was almost waiting. She was naturally clumsy, her self-consciousness made her more so, but yet she managed to avoid a disaster until the very end of the evening. Then, when the Duchess rose to go, she made a false step, stumbled, and revealed to her Grace, a Bishop, a member of Parliament, her two younger sisters, her father, and the rest of the room, the painful fact that she was in riding boots. Lord Northingbury behaved rather better than might have been expected; but from that day forth, while she remained at Crowborough, she never again rode to hounds.

That she remained at Crowborough so long was one of her misfortunes. She had the mortification of seeing both her sisters married before her, and when at last, at the age of thirty, she was taken by Lord Valerian, the relief seemed to have come too late. There was nothing left for her but to do her duty in that walk of life to which it had pleased God to call her – to be a blameless wife, a careful mother, and a respectable lady of title. So long as

Valerian was in the House, she withered dutifully through the seasons in London, like some transplanted vegetable; when at last he was turned out, it was with a sigh of relief that she finally involved herself in the long monotony of Sloanes. There she was in her native element; there she could breathe to the full the insipidity that was natural to her; there she could be dull, disappointed and irreproachable, from year's end to year's end. Her family alone provided her with a perpetual source of indifference. If, in the dry recesses of her spirit, she had ever harboured a dream, it was that she should bring forth a daughter – a daughter, whom she might lead along her own footsteps, and initiate, with complete propriety, into all the emptinesses of existence – a daughter who might be hers, and hers only, to rule over, to confide in, to look down upon, and to marry to the wrong man. But, as it happened, no daughter ever came. Instead, she gave birth to four sons, whom she could care for neither more nor less than she cared for their father. In her consciousness, in fact, they were simply an extension of Valerian; and her feelings towards that bulky, awkward, tiresomely harmless person, as each new image of him appeared, were merely, like a little butter on a large slice of bread, spread out a trifle thinner so that they might go round. Amid the solid mass of her indifference it was thus just possible to detect a faint infusion of hostility mingled with a dreary pride. Such was her attitude, not only towards her husband and her children, but towards everything to which she belonged. She disliked the estate and the people on it, because, with her clumsiness and her austerity, she was unpopular, because she dimly felt that it was she who was at fault, and because she had heard so often that the old Duchess had been adored. Yet she was proud of the great domain, with its wealth, its traditions, its celebrity, and the opportunities it offered for the exercise of power. The Duchess of Cheshire! She would be the Duchess of Cheshire! She thought of it with a kind of grey joy; but then, in a moment, the joy would vanish, leaving only the greyness upon her mind. After all, what was it to be a great lady? It was to labour under an endless load of obligations, and, however many attentions one might receive in return, never to receive enough. Besides, who could say how long it might not be before she came into her inheritance? Sometimes it almost seemed to her as if she never would. It seemed as if it was her fate to end as she had begun – in an eternal second place;

as if the Duke would continue through everlasting ages to grow older and older; as if Valerian would remain Valerian to the end of time; and as if she herself, with all the responsibilities and all the discomforts of sovereignty, would miss its glories as she had missed its secrets, passing as a servant still, and never as a mistress, through the bitter grandeur of her habitation and the perpetual disappointment of her life.

As she went down the Long Gallery with Lady Phyllis, these, as usual, were the undertones of her feeling, but her outward and obvious preoccupation was simply the wish to show things properly off. "The statues here were collected by the Duke's grandfather, when he was in Italy. Some of them have been photographed; and that is the famous Sloanes Apollo – the one without a head. Personally, I don't care for statues, do you?"

Lady Phyllis, who was interested in the arts, admired the draped figure on the left.

"Yes; but so few *are* draped. There was one here – oh! most shocking – I had to have it removed. How they'd allowed it to stay so long I can't think. It's true it was in one of the alcoves – rather out of sight; but then with children! I came on it quite by accident one day, and had the men in at once. It was so heavy they thought they'ld never be able to move it, but I insisted on their doing it somehow, and of course they did. It was very disagreeable. That cupid we got at Pompeii – Valerian wanted a momento – it was on our honeymoon tour."

Lady Phyllis hardly looked. She was still thinking of the statue that had to be taken away. "Why was it so very shocking?" she asked.

"Oh my dear! It was disgusting. The things they thought of then! It was" – Lady Valerian lowered her voice – "it was nearly life-size too!" And she led the way into the Queen's chamber.

The show rooms at Sloanes all lay in the great South Wing, which had been built at the beginning of the Eighteenth Century. The house was one of those huge buildings which, taken for granted in an English countryside, fill the heart of a foreign traveller with envy and amazement. It had grown up out of a remote antiquity, like some strange object of nature, slowly and spontaneously by a gradual process of accretion, accumulating within itself during the long passage of years the qualities of succeeding ages and the traces of a splendid past. A spectator could sweep into one glance of the eye a tower and a buttress of the twelfth century, a chapel by Inigo Jones, an early English dining hall, and a pavilion designed by Adam. At the heart of the house was an Elizabethan courtyard, glorious with red brick and mullioned window, two sides of which contained the famous library. The whole structure had been overhauled by Sir Christopher Wren. His master hand had joined with Time's to clothe diversity and harmony; and he had crowned his labours by the erection of the magnificent south façade which dominated the landscape of the park, and looked, across the terrace, the lawns, and the Italian garden, down the long elm avenue to the lake. Since his day, except for a few decorations by Adam there had been no further additions to Sloanes. The nineteenth century had done the best it could for the great house – it had left it alone; left it to mature in its own vast manner through the peace of the softly-slipping generations, to assume with each year, each month, each moment, some subtler shade of grandeur and of grace. The Twentieth Century had found it a thing as near perfection as it is given to any of man's works to be.

"Here are the two Claudes," said Lady Valerian, as she walked across the Queen's Chamber. "It was here that Queen Mary slept."

She passed rapidly with Lady Phyllis at her heels, through several small rooms, hung thickly with pictures in heavy frames, and furnished in the pompous style of the Eighteenth Century. As she went she pointed out a picture here and there, but Lady Phyllis never had time to do more than glance at it. "Guido's Faithful Shepherd – such a pretty thing. The Old Man is by Rembrandt; it was much admired by Lord Randolph Churchill. From this window you have a very good view of the lake." She hurried on, brushing past the boule cabinets and the colossal porcelain and the faded crimson curtains and the gilt chairs until they reached a larger and more highly decorated apartment. The arched ceiling was painted with gods and goddesses disporting in the azure; there were chandeliers and two elaborate mantelpieces; and, at the end of the room, filling the entire wall, was an immense Tintoretto – the celebrated Annunciation – which, brilliant, extraordinary, and over-flowing with tumultuous energy, seemed to open out a sudden miraculous vista into an incredible and enchanting world. Lady Valerian swept forward with her companion. "This, of course, is the Grand Saloon," she observed.

She walked straight to a table with a glass top. "That" – she pointed – "is a lock of King Charles's hair. There is nothing more in this room; now I must show you the Chapel."

Lady Phyllis was shown the Chapel, and the state dining-hall, and the vestibule with the armour of Sir Geoffrey Fiennes. At last she was taken upstairs to see Lady Valerian's bedroom. On the landing were two full-length pictures – a Gainsborough of the third Duchess with her little boy, and balancing it, a portrait of Lady Valerian, with Fiennes, by Ellis Roberts. "I think it's so nice to see them together," said Lady Valerian, opening the door of her bedroom.

The bedroom was fine and large. In the place of honour was a life-size painting of a colley-dog, with a distant view of a castellated mansion between its legs. On the gold mount were the words "Robin Adair". It represented Lady Valerian's favourite companion during her days at Crowborough. "Poor old fellow," she automatically murmured as she looked at it. "He won prizes at every show he went to." After being taken into the boudoir and shown the photographs, Lady Phyllis found that it was time to go. She declared that she could find her way down quite easily. "Turn to the right," said Lady Valerian. Lady Phyllis was feeling perverse, and turned to the left. A corridor seemed to lead into the older part of the house. She took it; went up some steps and down some others; turned several corners, and at last found herself in front of a large double door, surmounted by a coat of arms and elaborate carving in ancient oak. She was adventurous and inquisitive; the door was certainly far too grand for a bedroom; she turned the handle and went in.

COMMENTARY
"GODFREY, CORNBURY, OR CANDIDE?"

Strachey delivered this paper to the Apostles on 11 May 1912, a few months after the publication of *Landmarks in French Literature*. In his correspondence of this time, Strachey speaks of undergoing a "spiritual revolution", and it can be seen that, for him, consideration of the questions dealt with in this essay – happiness, duty, and ambition – was a necessary prelude to the development of social and political concern. In his memoir, "My Early Beliefs", Keynes discusses the effect of Moore's *Principia Ethica* on the Apostles of the year 1903, for whom "there was not a very intimate connection between 'being good' and 'doing good'; and we had a feeling that there was some risk that in practice the latter might interfere with the former". Keynes connects this feeling with the Apostles' neglect of those parts of *Principia Ethica* that deal with duty and correct behaviour. "Godfrey, Cornbury, or Candide?" shows that Strachey at least was beginning to consider these neglected issues.

The references to Godfrey and to Cornbury embody private jokes that Strachey's audience would have appreciated, for it was very bad form to make erudite allusions that could not be shared by all present; in fact, such un-Apostolic behaviour could merit a fine – payment for the next meeting's "whales". While it has not been possible to identify Godfrey, the representative of Epicureanism, it may be noted that Strachey's first name was Giles.

Henry Hyde (1710–53) whose disdain is equated with the ideal of self-sacrifice, was the son of the 3rd Earl of Clarendon. He bore the courtesy title of Viscount Cornbury, but was generally known as Lord Hyde after 1751 when he was summoned to the House of Lords in his father's barony. Following his death, Lady Mary Wortley Montagu spoke of his "very good heart", but added:

> I have often thought it a pity it was not under the direction of a better head.... On Lord Hyde's return from his travels, his

brother-in-law, the Lord Essex, told him with a great deal of pleasure, that he had got a pension for him. It was a very handsome one, and quite equal to his rank. All Lord Hyde's answer was "How could you tell, my Lord, that I was to be sold? or at least how could you know my price so exactly?" It was on this account that Mr Pope compliments him with that passage – "disdain what [ever] Cornbury disdains". [23 July 1753]

Leonard Woolf was in the Ceylon Civil Service from 1904 to 1911, when he resigned his post in order to marry Virginia Stephen. Maynard Keynes resigned from the India Office in 1908, after two years' service. He was appointed editor of the *Economic Journal* in 1911, and retained the editorship for thirty-three years.

Professor Green of Oxford was T. H. Green (1836–82), the famous neo-Hegelian philosopher who taught that self-determination requires consciousness of one's desires, and that freedom consists in a man's identifying himself with what he considers to be morally good.

GODFREY, CORNBURY, OR CANDIDE?

A God looks down upon this planet with a mild curiosity, and sees displayed before him mankind, moving and toiling, just as a man may look down upon the congregated activity of an ant-heap. But the speculations of the God are not quite analogous to those of the man. Ants, it is to be supposed, work simply and solely for their living; their purpose in life is the performance of those actions best calculated to promote the welfare of the ant-heap; and they go through those actions instinctively and remorselessly, without reflection and without individual desire. But the human heap works on a more complicated principle. The God looking down observes curiosities and ambiguities; strange motives seem to be at work, and things are done that fit into no system of Natural Selection. Can ever a God disentangle the meaning of all those movements, decide upon the aims of those variegated masses, explain or understand the directing purpose of the whole? Aim? Purpose? Is it possible to apply the words with any relevance in such a case? The God is confronted with a singular difficulty. The one thing that he sees with obvious certainty is the ceaseless energy of the heap; the one thing that remains mysterious is the result. The God takes on human shape, appears in the street, and asks the first passer-by what he is up to. The man is engaged in the trivial business of the day or its trivial pleasure, and his only thought beyond the affair of the moment is the earning of his livelihood; that is the one general consideration which underlies his actions; the mere ability to live is what justifies his life. "But why live?" the God asks. "Because I desire to live," the man replies, and can give no other answer. The God goes to a rich man's house. "What are *you* up to?" he inquires. The rich man gives a list of his engagements for the next day, the next week, the next year. "And after that?" – "After that I shall have more engagements." "And after those?" – "Still more." – "And then?" – "I shall die." – "And then?" – "I have no time to answer any more questions: I am already late. Good-bye." The God at last tries a member of the Apostles Club. – "Dearie, que fais-tu? Why all this agitation, this happiness this despair? Do try and give for once a rational answer. What *is* the point of your going on in the way you do – of your going on, in fact, at all?" And the reply of our brother. . .?

I don't think we sufficiently consider the question: for surely it is an important one. Doubtless we live in the main by instinct; but instincts are not absolutely inevitable; they may be over-ridden by reason. If we hold opinions as to the purpose of life, those opinions will probably affect our conduct; and the more we consider what those opinions should be, the more likely it is that reason will be our guide. It seems to me that we are too apt to take our premises for granted. We go on from day to day and year to year irreflectively, like parts of a machine; we gradually grow into our surroundings; we form habits; and at last we are fixed, more by chance than anything else, in a way of life whose merits we never seriously consider and whose significance we judge by petty standards of custom and convenience. It is difficult, no doubt, it is very difficult, to do anything else. For one thing, the majority of us are clogged by what seem to be the mere brute necessities of existence; we must make a living somehow, and if this is the only way –. Yet I think that we exaggerate even the power of those bonds. Careers *can* be thrown up. Woolf can refuse to go back to Ceylon, and Maynard can jump off his stool in London. These are refreshing instances; but they are rare, and perhaps after all delusory. Perhaps Woolf will idle away the rest of his days in parasitic incompetence; perhaps Maynard will be for ever proud of editing the *Economic Journal*. Well! At any rate they did make the attempt to re-shape their fortunes; they asked themselves what they were doing, and decided that it was not good enough, and that they must do something else. But I wonder what it was that made them come to their decision, – what it is that makes anyone come to a similar decision in a similar case.

To begin with, is it true that what really directs the course of life is the desire for pleasure? I think this may be the case. It certainly seems clear that hardly anyone at the present day would deliberately choose to live an unhappy life. Some degree of pleasure does appear to be with us a sine qua non. And I think that more than this is perhaps true – that considerations of pleasure form the really dominating factor in life. I do not mean that we are always trying to obtain the maximum of pleasure at every moment. I mean that on the whole by far the most important thing in life is our happiness; that, in general, we make all other aims subservient to the grand aim of acquiring as much happiness as we can. Other aims of course we have: We want to make other people happy, we want to do good, etc. etc. But, when it comes to one of those Woolf–Maynard crises of decision, how infinitely little are we affected by such aims! They are external supererogatory matters that weigh nothing with us. It is our own private happiness, and that alone, that counts. This I think, may not only be what actually happens, but it may also be the best thing that can happen: it is quite possible that the pursuit of one's own happiness is the right principle to go upon in life. To attend to our own pleasure may be the best way of promoting other people's. Isn't it possible? There is a charm, a serenity, about the Epicurean doctrine, which makes one wish, at any rate, that it were true. To sport with Godfrey in the sun! Ah! At least it pleases Godfrey as well as Giles.

Yet, if one veers towards the opposite extreme, how much there is to lure one! It is clear that the right principle to go upon is that which leads to the best result. We *ought* to do as much good as possible: very well then, let us set to work to do it, without more ado. Happiness may be a convenience, a necessity even; but what business have we to make it our first aim? Let us use it as the point of vantage from which we may lever up the world. I expect some people do act upon this principle – live laboriously to do good, and, having done good, die contented. When I consider, I begin to doubt whether after all we all don't – we at any rate *want* to live in some such way as that. To disdain what Cornbury disdains! If we could only manage it!

Only, if I look into my own heart, things seem to be different. What others think I can only conjecture, what I think I can at least dimly see. It seems to me that I live neither for happiness nor for duty. I like being happy, I scheme to be happy; I want to do my

duty, and I sometimes even do it. But such considerations seem
to affect me only sporadically and vaguely; there is something else
which underlies my actions more fundamentally, which guides,
controls, and animates the whole. It is ambition. I want to excel,
to triumph, to be powerful, and to glorify in myself. I do not
want a vulgar triumph, a vulgar power; fame and riches attract
me only as the subsidiary ornaments of my desire. What I want is
the attainment of a true excellence, the development of noble
qualities, and the full expression of them, – the splendour of a
spiritual success.

It is true that this is an egotistical conception of life; but I see no
harm in such an egotism. After all, each of us is the only person
who can cultivate himself; we may help on our neighbours here
and there – throw them a bulb or two over the garden wall, or
lend a hand with the roller; but we shall never understand the ins
and outs – the complication of the soils and the subsoils – in any
garden but our own. Nor even if we could, should we want to.
We really cannot be sufficiently interested in other people. But
Nature has provided us with a continuous, an unremitting, an
absorbing, an almost frantic interest in ourselves; well! let us
make the best use of it! And, if we do, if we cultivate our garden
to the utmost, there's at least a probability that our neighbour
too will profit in the end. Our surplus fruits will enrich the market,
and perhaps – who knows? – we may be lucky enough to produce some unique and wondrous blossom which the world would
never have enjoyed if it had not been for our long hours of self-
regarding care.

Am I right? I am still doubtful. – In the first place because my
theory seems to be perilously near to Professor Green of Oxford's
theory of "self-realization". But surely I wear mine with a difference? And secondly, I think that possibly – after all it is the ideal
of self-sacrifice – the disdain of Cornbury – that one *ought* to
follow, and perhaps actually would. It comes to this – Ought we
to be martyrs? It seems to me that there are occasions on which
we ought; and if so, doesn't it follow that we must be ready, if
things so fall out, to throw our ambition to the winds? All I can
say is that those occasions are very rare, and that therefore it is
useless to form a general theory of conduct upon them. It may
happen, by a strange concatenation of events, that the only decent
course for me to pursue is to be burned at the stake. But I think

one ought to regard such a denouement simply as an unpleasant accident.

But – martyr or no martyr – egoist or saint – philanthropist or voluptuary – when the funeral pyre is out and the last valediction over, how curious is the change that comes over the aspect of things! It is a strange inquiry to consider what remains of life when life is over. How irrelevant are our achievements to the efforts that brought them forth! What have the greatest of us to do with their works? Frederick re-drew the map of Europe and changed the destinies of nations, but Frederick himself –? Where is it – that odd entanglement of agitations which made up what was indeed his life? If you could catch his disembodied spirit, and show it the map of Europe redrawn and the nations with their changed destinies, would it not thank you for nothing? It was not the results of his greatness that he cared for; it was his greatness itself. And that –? – There is a comfortless kind of disproportion between the little row of volumes that make up the works of Shakespeare and Shakespeare's actual life. The man did that, it is true; but it was not to do that that he lived; it was for something different, for something far more personal; and one feels that if that is all that has come of it, he has been somewhat cheated. Oh, if one could only live for the glory of God! If one could find eternal crowns hereafter, and reconciliations and fulfilments in the bosom of Christ! But that sort of thing is no longer done. Crowns are no longer worn, and heaven is out of fashion. – Tout cela est bien vrai disait Candide, mais il faut cultiver notre jardin.

Men, Women, Sex and Art

COMMENTARY
"WILL IT COME RIGHT IN THE END?"

This late Apostle's paper, whose themes are similar to those of "Art and Indecency", can be dated 1908 or later on the evidence of its reference to "Mr Birrell". Francis Birrell (1889–1935), an old Etonian who went up to King's in 1908, was a critic and journalist; he was the son of Augustine Birrell, chief secretary for Ireland until the Easter Rebellion of 1916, and renowned man of letters. A friend of Strachey and many of the Bloomsbury set, it was "Frankie" Birrell who occasioned D. H. Lawrence's famous dream of "black beetles". Rupert Brooke, who is mentioned in the same passage in this paper, went up to King's in 1906.

The Milton quotation is from Book IX of *Paradise Lost*. "Mr Strachey on Mr Wells" refers to Lytton Strachey's cousin, St Loe Strachey, the very conservative editor of the *Spectator*, who was later to provide Lytton with employment as a reviewer. Harley Granville-Barker (1877–1946) was an actor, producer, playwright, critic, and great friend of George Bernard Shaw. "Mr Archer" was William Archer (1856–1924), a critic and journalist who campaigned for the abolition of theatre censorship and the formation of a national theatre. Edward Carpenter (1844–1929) was the eccentric socialist writer and devoted friend of Walt Whitman who gave up his Trinity Hall, Cambridge fellowship and resigned from holy orders to take up market-gardening and sandal-making. In 1894 he delivered and subsequently published a daring lecture on homosexuality called *Homogenic Love*. "Mr Redford", the villain of the piece, was George Alexander Redford (d. 1916), who was Examiner of plays from 1895–1911, after having served as a bank manager for many years.

WILL IT COME RIGHT IN THE END?

This is not the question I want the Society to answer, though no doubt it may if it likes; the question I'm really interested in is not "*Will* it come right in the end?" but "*Can* it?" I want to know if the World really is suffering under an ineradicable curse, if man has really fallen, or if on the other hand all that has happened is that things have grown confused and that there is hope of a second Eden after all. But it is too late, or too early, to be ambitious; and I am only anxious at the present moment to clear up a *part* of the problem of evil. Perhaps, though, the most important part. When the apple was eaten, everyone knows what was the first most obvious and remarkable result.

> As with new wine intoxicated both,
> They swim in mirth, and fancy that they feel
> Divinity within them breeding wings
> Wherewith to scorn the Earth. But that false fruit
> Far other operation first displayed,
> Carnal desire inflaming. He on Eve
> Began to cast lascivious eyes; she him
> As wantonly repaid; in lust they burn.

In short, the first form of wickedness is lasciviousness. Many persons would agree that this was so; and nearly everyone would agree that, if it is a form of wickedness at all, it is also the most difficult to get rid of. In spite of the progress of medical science, mankind seems to be no nearer now than it was in the days of Sir Thomas Browne to the happy art of propagating like a tree; we must still be content – and so far as can be seen we shall always have to be content – with the rough and ready method of carnal copulation. And, so long as this is the case, it seems clear that one of the essential attributes of mankind must be lasciviousness. We may do our best to regulate this lasciviousness; we may tighten up the law of divorce, and struggle to copulate not more than once a week; but the fact remains that we shall still copulate, and that we shall still enjoy copulating, however wicked that may be. If the human race is to continue, that is to say if all that we know of goodness and beauty is to continue, we must fuck. It *is* lust that makes the world go round.

Lust, then, is necessary; and thus it follows that, if it is also evil, the universe can never be absolutely good. But *is* it evil? That is the question that interests me, partly because I am naturally interested in the reputation of the universe, and partly because the question in itself opens up such singular vistas, and seems so queer and complicated and difficult to answer. Indeed, to judge from the number and the variety of the answers that are perpetually being given, it would seem as if this question were one of the most extraordinary that could possibly be put. It has the same sort of effect on people as the golden syrup of Habdul-Balbek, which (as the Society will remember) might turn the man who drank it into an angel, or a pig, or a jibbering idiot, or a woman, or might have no effect on him at all. One has only to read the evidence in the Censorship Commission or the Divorce Commission, one has only to read Mr Strachey on Mr Wells, or Mr Swinburne on Sappho, one has only to go to London and interview one's medical man, or walk into King's and talk to Mr Brooke or Mr Birrell, to realize what preposterously different answers to this one question different people will give. I shall try, however, in order to make the points at issue plainer, to classify these different answers; and I think it is easy to see that there are certainly three, and possibly four, main divisions into which they fall. But first I must settle a matter of nomenclature. The word most commonly used whenever discussions of this kind begin is the word "indecent", and it is always assumed that the meaning of this word is not in dispute. It is assumed that to call a thing "indecent" is to mean that it is (a) lascivious and (b) bad. The word is generally accepted as a term of abuse. There is no harm in this, so long as it is not *also* used as a term of mere description – a term implying simply that a thing is lascivious, without

73

determining whether it is good or bad; and the fact that it *is* often used in this double sense seems to be the cause of some confusion. If it were true that whatever is lascivious is bad, there would be no difficulty; but that is precisely the question at issue. To call a thing indecent because it is lascivious is to beg the question; to deny that a thing is lascivious because it is not indecent is a non sequitur. I shall try, therefore, always to use "indecent" to mean both bad and lascivious, and "lascivious" to imply nothing as to goodness or badness at all.

The largest class of persons who argue on this subject – the official class it may be called – hold that, as a matter of fact, all lasciviousness *is* bad, and therefore indecent. This class includes the average Englishman, – Mr Redford is the most obvious example –, who believes, whatever his conduct may be, or his conversation, that in every case (with one single exception) lasciviousness is an evil, in varying degrees of course, but still always an evil – a thing which every good man does his utmost to repress, and would like to see completely rooted out. He goes further than this, because he considers not only that lasciviousness itself, but everything associated with lasciviousness, is indecent. He would be shocked and disgusted if he saw two naked persons copulating in the street; but his shock and his disgust are only one or two degrees less violent when he hears of obstetrical instruments or venereal diseases or scientific inquiries into the nature of sex. The single exception which these officials make in their sweeping condemnation is in the case of a man and woman united in lawful wedlock, and coming together in a double bed. The fact that this exception is universally made appears to be quite certain, and it is most important. To assert that the copulation of a husband and wife is an indecent act would be considered highly paradoxical, and yet it must be allowed that such a copulation is lascivious. Thus the vast majority of persons agree that it is at least *possible* that lasciviousness should not be bad.

The second class is the Advanced class, though how far it is advanced is doubtful. It is this class that contains our leading writers and critics. Mr Granville Barker, for instance, and Mr Archer; and its main object appears to be to combat the extreme views of the officials. It is concerned chiefly with showing that it is untrue to say that everything associated with lasciviousness is indecent. It argues, for instance, that there need be nothing

74

indecent in a play written on the subject of an illegal operation. But the method of argument seems to imply that the Advanced class agrees with the official class that lasciviousness itself is always indecent, for it takes the form of pointing out that what is associated with lasciviousness is not in itself lascivious, and that *therefore* it is not indecent; so that the implication is that it *would* be indecent if it were lascivious and that therefore what is lascivious is bad. But it is difficult to be quite certain about the views of the Advanced class; nor are they particularly interesting. Their main point – that the extremes of officialdom are absurd – is so obviously true that it is platitudinous; and on the general question they are vague.

But on the whole it seems fairly certain that if the world were composed entirely of the official and the advanced, lasciviousness itself would be, if not in practice at least in theory, universally condemned. Everyone would agree that the Music Halls *ought* to be suppressed, and that the Restoration Comedies are a disgrace to the English stage. A bill making the wearing of bathing-drawers a penal offence would receive no support either in the House of Commons or the Country; and the greatest reform that could be hoped for would be the withdrawal of the prohibition against the performance of *Ghosts*. However, as a matter of fact, there is another class in existence whose views are hostile to the official views and distinct from the Advanced – the class of Naturalists. In their opinion it is impossible to condemn what is natural; copulation, nudity, etc., are clearly natural; they therefore cannot be bad, and in fact, since the performance of natural functions is good as a means, these functions must be approved of. It is as senseless to blame a man for copulating as for blowing his nose, they say or seem to say, for their utterances are not always lucid. It seems certain at any rate that Mr Edward Carpenter, for instance, would assert that a great number of things considered indecent by the official class were really decent. It is less certain whether he has any good reason for doing so. It is not reasonable to excuse copulation on the ground of its being a natural function, because there is obviously one point in which it differs from other natural functions, and it is upon this very point that the whole question depends. The difference is that the *act* of copulation is accompanied by violent feelings, while the act of blowing one's nose is accompanied by none; and the question is whether these feelings – these feelings of lasciviousness – are bad or not. To approve them because *they* as well as the act are natural seems a shady line to take. Who can say what feelings are natural and what are not? Clearly the mere fact of feelings accompanying natural acts does not make them so. But probably if the naturalists were pushed as far as this they would try to wriggle out by differentiating between the various feelings which accompany lascivious acts. Some they would declare were natural, honest, healthy feelings; others they would say were contorted, morbid, and depraved; and they might possibly add that it was only the latter which were really lascivious. They might deny that when a healthy male copulates with a healthy female, the feelings aroused were really lascivious at all. It is only a corrupt civilization which makes them so. If that is their argument they ought perhaps to be considered merely a branch of the Advanced class. It is true that they would be in favour of prohibiting bathing-drawers, but that would be, not because they were in favour of lasciviousness, but because they considered nudity was *not* lascivious, and, as they might add, bathing-drawers were really *more* lascivious – more *suggestive*. And for the same reasons they would eagerly join in the prohibition of the Restoration plays.

They might take that line, or on the other hand they might boldly assert that no feelings accompanying natural acts could be bad, and that therefore, though those feelings were no doubt usually lascivious they were not indecent. They might say that the whole conception of lasciviousness being anything to be ashamed of was a dream and a delusion, and that the sooner society returns to the condition of indiscriminate copulation the better. That is a sweeping theory, and therefore an attractive one. But it has two flaws – in the first place it depends upon the not very brilliant distinction between what is natural and what is unnatural; and in the second place it is contradicted by the views of a respectable and ever-increasing body of people – the Bawdy class.

At first sight it may seem odd that this class – of which I am proud to acknowledge myself a member – should hold views incompatible with any which look upon the shamefulness of lasciviousness as a delusion, and indiscriminate copulation as the ideal state. Yet on reflection it becomes plain that this must be so. The attitude of the Bawdy class towards lasciviousness is neither that of approval nor of disapproval; it is that of amusement. They laugh, and that is quite enough. But, if it is true that copulation and all the feelings connected with it are as ordinary and harmless as breathing and eating and blowing one's nose, what on earth are they laughing at? Why are they not always making jokes about sneezes, and whispering absurd asides about the pulsations of the heart? The reply might be that what they are really laughing at are not the acts or the feelings themselves, but the ridiculous opinions usually held about them. If people had the sense to see that lasciviousness was as innocent as going to sleep, it would be a very different matter. Precisely; far too different; for, in that case, on that theory, their jokes would stop. If the naturalist view was the true one, and the world were converted to it, the Bawdy class would simply disappear; it would have nothing to laugh at; its occupation would be gone. But really, who can seriously suppose that the Bawdy class ever will or ever could disappear? The foolish opinions of other people may add a flavour to the joke, but the joke is there, whatever other people think. And, if the joke is there, there must be *something* queer about lasciviousness; the naturalists are wrong. Are then the officials right? But the officials also cannot be right, so long as there *is* a joke. The officials deny, in their theory, that there's any joke – though they may, in practice, titter; the whole thing, according to them, is no fit subject for mirth – it is indecent, deplorable, and bad. And yet the fact remains that they do titter; even the advanced class titters occasionally; the Naturalists, it is true, never titter, but then it is well known that they have no sense of humour; and as for the Bawdy, they are ex hypothesi, laughing all the time.

On the whole, in fact, there is good reason to suppose that bawdy jokes are good jokes. But their curious characteristic is that they would not be good unless they were *about* something which was, somehow or other, bad. I mean by a good joke a joke that it is good to contemplate; and it seems to me that the essence of good bawdy jokes is simply a matter of arrangement – that they arrange what is unbecoming in a becoming way. The bawdy joke is only really good when it produces the perception both of something unbecoming and of that something arranged charmingly, so that its nature is curiously transmuted – its nastiness preserved in an unexpected exquisite surrounding, like a fly in amber. If that's true, it gives a clue to the nature of lasciviousness, for it follows that lasciviousness is not in itself either good or bad, but that its value depends on its surroundings. Its presence may make one organic whole bad, and another good, and another simply indifferent. I think this is the true view and that it explains the discordance on the subject among the numbers of my first three classes. If they recognized that the mere fact of proving a thing to be lascivious proved nothing at all as to its value, they might come to some agreement. "Mr Swinburne's poems are indecent!" exclaim the officials. "Indecent!" echo the advanced in horror, "how can you say so? Can't you see how beautiful they are?" "We say nothing about their beauty", reply the officials. "What we do say is – look at them, and then pretend if you dare that they're not reeking with semen and erections and sadisms, that they're not horribly lascivious in fact, just as the lowest and vulgarest of music halls is lascivious – there's precisely the same element in both." And, so far as I can see, the only rejoinder as yet discovered by the Advanced is to accuse the officials of having dirty minds – which is no doubt true, but it does not leave them with the best of the argument. Their real rejoinder is, on my theory, quite simple. It is to admit to the full the presence of lasciviousness in Mr Swinburne, and to add that it is owing to that very fact that his poems are valuable. But I'm afraid it will be a long time before the Advanced class ever do say anything as bright as that.

But I should like to examine more closely the nature of these wholes of which lasciviousness forms a part. And first it is neces- sary to distinguish those which are acts or objects from those which are feelings, for it is clear that it is only the feelings which can be properly said to be good or bad in themselves. And as to lascivious feelings, one of the reasons for supposing that they are nearly always bad seems to be that a great number of feelings which are really lascivious are not recognized as being so, while it is understood that they are good. Thus very many of our feelings towards beautiful persons, either existing or represented, are tinged with lasciviousness; and, though everyone admits that these feelings are good, their lasciviousness is hardly ever realized. Similarly the ordinary man is very unwilling to admit that there may be an element of lust in love. The goodness of lascivious feelings seems to depend on the same sorts of qualities which determine the goodness of other feelings – such qualities as straightforwardness, and refinement, and an appreciation of how much is enough; and the bad lascivious feelings bear the same sort of relation to the good ones as sentimentality does to affection: – the difference is immense and obvious, but it cannot be described. The lascivious wholes which are simply *objects* of consciousness must I suppose be considered aesthetically – as beautiful or ugly – as things of which the contemplation is good or bad. But I am not sure whether they are really always aesthetic in the ordinary sense. Sometimes no doubt they are – Mr Swinburne's poems, for instance; but is the value of a good improper story aesthetic? And, on the other hand, can one say that a vulgar and indecent Music Hall turn is simply ugly? There seems to be some curious un-recognized tract of territory somewhere between morals and aesthetics, where the values depend on a queer intermixture of both – on such things as good taste and a kind of intellectual elegance and vigour on one side and vulgarity and a sort of silli-ness and insignificance on the other. But at any rate it does seem clear that the value of these wholes depends on some element of *appropriateness* between the parts. And the wholes appear to me to be often very complex – including an immense number of sur-rounding circumstances of time and place and occasion and accompanying states of mind. And it is this fact – this complexity and subtlety in the nature of lascivious objects – which it seems to me is one of the main causes of the confusion of opinion about them. In particular it helps to explain the rigours and furies of the official class – their wholesale condemnation of lasciviousness. And this is so because when one is thinking of some past lascivious act it is exceedingly difficult – and for the official, almost impos-sible – to call up the entire mass of its surroundings; and it is upon these surroundings that a right judgement of its value depends. When one sits down to consider copulation in a cool hour, what happens? One roughly inserts a perception of its bleak physical acts and feelings into the middle of the calm and sober atmosphere of a reflective mood. In the middle, so to speak, of a song by Brahms, one take down one's trowsers and shows an erection; the result is shocking, not to say disgusting. But this is not giving copulation a fair chance. To do that one must conjure up a whole world of strange excitements, gradually beginning and mys-teriously deepening, one must imagine the shock and the pressure of bodies, and realize the revelation of an alien mind, one must find oneself familiar with miracles and, assuming an amazing triumph, swim in glory through a palpitating universe of heavenly and unimaginable lust. By poetry and by music one can reach this frame of mind, and thus to the ordinary man the lasciviousness of Romeo and Juliet or of [lacuna in manuscript] comes with nothing of a shock. And, in the only occasion in common life in which he is able, by habit or association, to grasp the true atmosphere of a lascivious whole – in the copulation of husband and wife – he can see at once that it is not indecent.

But this is an exception; and the result on the whole of the mistakes (and no doubt also the superstitions) of the ordinary man is I think that an immense number of lascivious wholes which are really valuable in themselves have been crushed out of existence. It seems to me certain that the Athenians were infinitely wiser in this respect than Mr Redford. Mr Redford's error is that he persists in confusing aesthetics with morals. If he realized that it is absurd to attempt to put down indecency as it would be to attempt to put down bad painting, he would resign his office. And the reason why it is absurd to put down bad painting is a purely practical one – it is, as a matter of fact, impossible to devise rules by which you really *only* put down the painting that is bad. You may seem to achieve an obvious benefit by shutting up the Royal Academy, but if you do that you will find, when it comes to the point, that you have started on a career of suppression which will end with the stamping out of all originality and experiment in art. For this reason, when the Advanced class protest against the "Library Censorship", and at the same time support the act against indecent publications, they show that they have failed to grasp the elements of the situation. If good literature is to flourish it is absolutely essential that there should be no restraint upon literature that is bad. The same rule applies to conduct; and the only hope of our ever getting a really beautiful and vigorous and charming civilization is to allow the whole world to fuck and bugger and abuse themselves in public and generally misbehave to their hearts' content.

Am I simplifying? I don't know; but I feel pretty sure that the main outlines are correct. And if I am, there does seem at any rate some possibility of it's coming right in the end. There's no need for an entire change in the nature of man; all he needs is honesty, wisdom, courage, and good taste, in order to put the whole business on a satisfactory basis. But when he has done that, the world will be singularly changed. I seem to see the Hermae rising once more at the street-corners, and to hear the astounding laughter of a subtler and huger Aristophanes. I seem to dwell among new braveries and absurdities and fascinations, to come smiling into surprising paradises, and to experience serenely God knows how many extraordinary loves.

COMMENTARY
"ART AND INDECENCY"

This piece bears no date, but its thematic similarity to the late Apostle's paper, "Will It Come Right in the End?" makes it probable that it was written at the same time – sometime before 1908. It employs some of the distinctions used in the other paper, and its style seems suitable for delivery to one of the several Cambridge societies to which Strachey belonged. The central argument of the essay is today something of a critical commonplace, but it is expressed with a wit and elegance that more than justifies its publication. Strachey's argument relies on the principle of organic unity which he has adapted from G. E. Moore. The reader may care to compare the last paragraph of Strachey's piece with the following passage from Moore's *Principia Ethica*:

> It is to be observed that beautiful objects are themselves, for the most part, organic unities, in this sense, that they are wholes of great complexity, such that the contemplation of any part, by itself, may have no value, and yet that, unless the contemplation of the whole includes the contemplation of that part, it will lose in value. [p. 202]

ART AND INDECENCY

The question that I want to discuss is partly aesthetic and partly moral: exactly how much of one and how much of the other, it is difficult to say. In general, the relation between aesthetics and ethics is apt to be confused. On the one hand, it seems clear that a work of art ought to be judged as a work of art, and as nothing else; that is to say, its value must be determined upon purely aesthetic grounds – just as the value of a dinner must be determined upon culinary grounds, and that of a steam-engine upon considerations of engineering. It would be absurd to praise a locomotive for its virtue, or to condemn a soup as immoral; and it seems no less absurd to discuss the ethics of a symphony. Conversely, it is ridiculous to introduce aesthetic considerations into moral questions; the Kaiser's delinquencies have really nothing to do with his moustaches; and, while it is probable that some at any rate of the 11,000 virgins of Cologne were not good-looking, their holiness remains unimpeachable. So far, then, "art for art's sake" appears to be a reasonable proposition. But two provisos must be made. In the first place, it is no doubt true that the *effects produced* by a work of art may be of an ethical nature. It would be unnecessarily sceptical to doubt this; for there does not seem to be any specific quality in works of art which should exempt them from producing results of this kind. If men are capable of being made better or worse by forces outside themselves, there is no reason to exclude from those forces literature, painting, and music. The Bible is fine poetry: but it would be paradoxical to deny that its dissemination has produced moral results (of one kind or another) of the highest importance. It is, however, equally clear that it is impossible to estimate the moral effects of any work of art apart from a great number of particular circumstances. No general rule can be laid down; what is one man's meat is another man's poison; many clergymen who have read Catullus with impunity, have been, it is reported, completely demoralized by Mrs Humphry Ward. Time, place, age, nationality, character, the accidents of mood and temper, all these, together with innumerable other concomitant facts, must be taken into account in every case. And, when the account has been made up and the balance struck, it is important to remember that the resulting judgement is *not* a judgement on the work of art itself, but simply on its effects. The distinction, though it is sometimes overlooked, is really fundamental. In what follows, I shall make no attempt to deal with this side of the question – the question of ethical effects.

But there is another, and a more direct, way in which ethics and aesthetics are related. It is certain that *ethical constituents* are often to be found in works of art. In many tragedies, to take an obvious example, questions of right and wrong, of good and evil, are of very great importance. The wickedness of Iago is a vital part of *Othello*. It is, therefore, impossible to maintain that ethical considerations are necessarily irrelevant to art; and when the phrase "art for art's sake" is intended to cover such a proposition, it is false. Among the many and varied elements which go to the making of works of art, ethical elements sometimes occur. These ethical elements, however, are parts of an aesthetic whole; and the aesthetic whole must be judged by purely aesthetic standards. In this sense, "art for art's sake" expresses the true doctrine.

These general remarks may I hope simplify the discussion of the particular question, or group of questions, that I wish to put before you – namely, is there any peculiar relation between the artistic and the indecent, and if there is, what is it? The question is highly controversial, and has been approached from a great many points of view; but the main currents of opinion are fairly easily discernible. There are three classes of persons whose views upon the subject are pronounced and completely incompatible. The first of these classes is an extremely respectable one – the class of prudes. The prudes regard with horror, detestation, and anger any introduction of indecency into works of art. They are not only a respectable, but a busy race. In their time, they have done a

great deal. They have affixed fig-leaves to the statues of the Gods
of Antiquity, they have draped the posteriors of Michael Angelo's
devils, they have bowdlerized Shakespeare, and prohibited the
performance of the *Oedipus Rex*. They are, however, diminishing
both in numbers and in assurance. They seem never to have
recovered from the loss which they sustained on the death of
Queen Victoria. Ever since that sad event, they have fallen sick
of a grievous malady: they have begun to compromise. Now a
prude who compromises is a prude lost. The whole strength of his
position lies in its rigidity: (it is like a maidenhead – either all
there, or not there at all). Mr Bowdler was inexpugnable.
Shakespeare contains indecencies; indecency is bad: the inference
is obvious: remove the indecencies, and you will improve
Shakespeare. Mr Bowdler did so, and Queen Victoria was satis-
fied; but her degenerate successors are not. They have quietly
abandoned Mr Bowdler, and in so doing they have let the enemy
into their citadel. For once admit that there are any exceptions –
that there is a single exception – to the golden rule of prudery: –
"all indecency is bad, of whatever kind and in whatever
circumstances" – and you will find that you are slipping down an
inclined plane which may land you in heaven knows what
alarming position. If Shakespeare is really better with his indecencies than without them, may not the same be said of Swift? and if
it be true of Swift, then why not of Rabelais? And if Rabelais is
tolerated, surely it is straining at a gnat and swallowing a camel to
disapprove of the Restoration dramatists. It is possible, no doubt,
to refine and to distinguish to construct whole elaborate casuis-
tries of indecency; but such theorizings seem to be based on no
definite principles, and to differ in the most divergent ways
according to individual taste. Thus at the present time the party
of the prudes presents a spectacle of the utmost confusion.
Without the golden rule of Victoria they resemble, in incoherence
and multiplicity, the Protestant sects after their rejection of the
infallibility of Rome. Among the various groups of prudes that
one meets with, there is no criterion for deciding which are the
orthodox. There are some who are disgusted by the tittering
flippancy of Sterne, but who relish the honest coarseness of
Fielding; there are others who find Fielding barbarous, but are
edified by the realism of Zola. Some, who put Giorgione's
Concert over their mantel pieces, turn away in horror from

Manet's *Déjeuner sur L'Herbe*; while the authorities, who hang Bronzius's *Venus and Cupid* on the walls of the National Gallery, conceal Michael Angelo's *Leda* in the cellar. One finds a learned divine, who is appalled when Renan writes on the ethics of passion, translating with infinite labour into the purest English the truly shocking Dialogues of Plato. At the same time the official censor of stage plays, while he protects the diluted ineptitudes of Parisian salaciousness, declares in tones of thunder that there are two subjects which may never, never, be referred to in any theatre – Jesus Christ and incest.

It is not surprising that there has been a reaction against this curiously confused and wavering creed; and the form of the reaction was almost inevitable in a scientific generation. The majority of advanced thinkers on the subject fall into my second class, and may be appropriately called the Naturalists. To them, the whole question of indecency is simplified in a fundamental manner, because, in their opinion, there is really no such thing. Indecency does not exist. It is a superstition, a myth – the result of a mixture of barbarous and ignorant tradition and the artificialities of civilization, of erroneous education and a confused association of ideas. The acts which are popularly called indecent – the acts of reproduction, of excretion, and so forth, are – so the Naturalists affirm – indistinguishable from the other bodily functions. They are necessary, natural acts, and it is as absurd to attach ethical qualities to them as it would be to attach ethical qualities to eating or blowing one's nose – for instance – to the emission of seminal fluid from a penis as it would be to attach them to the emission of mucous fluid from a nose. "All this fuss about a little bit of flesh!" the Naturalists seem to exclaim; though it is true that the word "flesh" would be hardly to their liking; they would prefer to speak, less figuratively, of "the sexual instinct". For it is a noticeable peculiarity of theirs that they have a great love of latinized locations; and the reason for this is obvious: there is something detached and scientific in such expressions as "coitus", "fellatio", or "homosexualist" which is lacking in the more coloured phraseology of familiar speech, and which makes them therefore more appropriate to the naturalistic way of thinking. Such being their views, the Naturalists, when asked what in their opinion was the relation between the artistic and the indecent, would reply that the whole question was without

significance; that, as the very notion of "indecency" was a falla-
cious one, it was absurd to suppose that the merit of a work of art
would be affected by the presence or the absence of it; and they
would probably add some regrets that a foolish superstition
should discourage the artistic presentation of various psychologi-
cal and medical truths of great importance – such as, for instance,
the excretory aberrations of infants, or the unpleasant consequences of venereal infection.

Now there can, I think, be little doubt that the naturalistic view
of the case has much to recommend it. It is simple, and it is
decidedly advanced; and if one were obliged to choose between it,
and the view of the prudes, most thoughtful and unbiased
inquirers would probably declare for the Naturalists. But these
two opinions are not the only alternatives. There is a third party –
a class whose sentiments are apt to be overlooked, for they have
no high pretensions and, as a rule, they are without the habit of
philosophical disquisition; yet they are a large, and even an
influential class – the class of the Bawdy. The superior person,
from his moral or intellectual eminence, may affect to look down
upon the Bawdy; but are they in reality to be despised? In the
first place, it must not be forgotten that among this class are to be
reckoned some of the very greatest of the human race – Aristophanes, Rabelais, Voltaire. And then, is it possible to put on one
side and treat as of no account the predilections of the multitudes
who, through so many ages, have been moved to admiration and
delight by the works of those masters, and of many more who
belong to the same category? The prim Victorians who were
shocked by Charlotte Brontë were no doubt, in one sense, highly
respectable; but the loose Elizabethans who shook their sides over
the solid lewdnesses of Ben Jonson were, perhaps, respectable
in another sense – that is to say they deserved to be respected. At
any rate, it is certain that between these two classes – the prudes
and the bawdy – there can be no agreement; they are naturally
exclusive. But it is no less certain that the opposition is equally
fundamental between the bawdy and the Naturalists. For, if the
Naturalists are right, the whole basis of the bawdy standpoint is
destroyed. If indeed there is no such thing as indecency, Aristophanes, Rabelais, Voltaire, are undoubtedly the most futile of the
writers, their jests are meaningless, and their admirers are bamboozled fools. This certainly seems a paradoxical conclusion;

and the question arises whether the premises of the Naturalists will really support it. Now the naturalistic argument rests, as we have seen, on the contention that the acts usually termed indecent are merely natural acts, and that there is therefore no reason to put them in a special category. Suppose we admit this, what follows? Surely nothing; for is it not clear that, however we describe the acts, the real point at issue is concerned, far less with the acts themselves, than with the feelings accompanying them? It is upon the feelings, and not upon the acts, that we base our judgement when we assert something to be indecent; it is, in short, a state of mind that we are considering, not a state of body. To do otherwise is to commit the fallacy of those amiable educationists who blandly set out to teach their little charges the "mysteries of sex" by means of diagrams illustrating the secretive properties of glands, or a few short lessons on the functions of stamens and pistils. Alas! the "mysteries of sex" do not lie there. You might as well try to describe the nature of war by means of the plans of battlefields. It is not at all a question of properties and functions, or of glands and ducts, or of movements of living tissue: it is a question of mental states – of extraordinary agitations, of unexpected and dominating impulses, of intensifying excitements, of unparalleled joys; and the young pupil who has no acquaintance with these sensations knows no more of the "mysteries of sex" than the young soldier knows of war who has never been in action. And it is for this reason that the latinized vocabulary affected by the Naturalists must be regarded with suspicion. For, in spite of its air of detachment, it is in reality a means of concealing the actual facts. The Saxon words, with their emotional associations, are far more truthful. What could be more unaffecting than the expression "coitus"? But the reality, which it designates, is not unappetizing at all.

Thus the case of the Naturalists, owing to their failure to realize that indecency depends on feelings and not on acts, appears to break down. Are we then to throw ourselves without more ado into the arms of the bawdy? Perhaps it would be wise to pause; for they are a reckless, *tête-montée*, and not at all philosophical race. They are apt to defend their doings upon totally incompatible grounds. Nothing is commoner than to find them when they are attacked by the prudes for indecency, exclaiming loudly, and in tones of outraged innocence, that they are *not* indecent, that they have been monstrously misunderstood, it is the prudes who have dirty minds, not they, that *they* have been only anxious to inculcate the highest virtues, if only the prudes would take the trouble to read them aright. A famous instance of this line of defence may be seen in Dryden's and Vanburgh's replies to the attacks of Jeremy Collier. On the other hand, at other moments, their argument is very different. Indecency, they seem to say, is a positive merit in art; we will have just as much of it as we like, and if that is a good deal more than *you* like – well, so much the worse for you. Such is the attitude of the French decadents of the last century. Clearly these views are mutually destructive. But is the bawdy case capable of a more satisfactory defence?

First, it seems certain that the *extreme* bawdy position is untenable. It is surely possible that in some cases the merit of a work of art may be decreased by indecency. It is easy to think of pornographic works which have no artistic merit and of Music Hall revues which would be artistically improved by the deletion of the feeble indecencies which they contain. But, on the other hand, the *extreme* prude position is equally impossible. A work of art which is indecent may be of the highest merit. Between these two extremes, what sort of a middle course can we steer?

The view I suggest is that works of art must be considered as complex wholes, composed of a great number of parts; the value of these wholes cannot be determined merely by a *sum* of the values of the parts, but depends upon their *combination*. That wholes of this kind exist it is easy to see. A whole, for instance, consisting of the pleasurable contemplation of a beautiful object is made up of two parts – the pleasurable contemplation, and the beautiful object. Now a beautiful object, in isolation, is probably almost valueless; and mere pleasurable contemplation, directed towards no particular object is of small value; yet the two to-gether form a whole of very great value indeed. Now, if as I believe, works of art are wholes of this nature, it is obvious that to consider the value of their parts in isolation is futile: it will give no indi-cation of the total value of the whole. A part which, in isolation, might be of purely negative value, might in combination, form a whole of high merit. Remove it, and though it is valueless in itself, its absence will destroy the value of the whole. Indecency, when it appears in works of art, seems to me to be a part of this nature. It is impossible to determine its value apart from the combination of which it forms a part. The value of some wholes may be decreased by its presence; but the value of others may be immeasurably increased; and indeed its presence may be absolutely vital to the value of a work of art. This theory I think affords an explanation of the curiously conflicting views that obtain on the subject. Indecent feelings, indecent acts, when considered in isolation are very liable to appear in an odious light. They strike the cool observer as out of place; they are inappropriate to his surroundings; they are shocking in fact; combined with the rest of his state of mind – the state of mind of the unemotional onlooker – they form a complex whole which is unpleasant and ugly, and he therefore condemns them as bad. But, place these same indecencies in another complex whole – in a work of art, – in which they are fitted to their surroundings, in which they are gradually led up to and elaborated, so that the observer, no longer cool, no longer unemotional, feels, sympathizes, and understands – then the case is altered: the dull and horrid image of a sensualist's imagination becomes the vital element of some radiant creation – one of the poems of Catullus, one of the comedies of Congreve, of Tristram Shandy, of Candide.

COMMENTARY
"HE, SHE, AND IT"

"He" and "She" are the characters in this dialogue, and "It" is the subject. In the discussion of sexual roles in this little piece, opinions are advanced that are remarkably congenial to feminists of our own era, and the comic device of making the speakers hypothetically switch gender adds poignancy to the expression of those opinions. Ostensibly, the central issue of the dialogue is women's suffrage, but that is quickly swallowed up by questions about the influence of education and nurture on women's own conception of their social role.

The treatment of these questions seems very like the one to be found in today's newspaper, and it is astonishing to realize that the date of composition of this piece is 20 February 1904. Near the end of the piece Strachey seems to have wavered in his purpose, and the whole thing seems to become a work of homosexual apology; but perhaps the author has his tongue in his cheek, and does not really mean the rather trivial introduction of pederasty into the argument to detract from its main theme, which is clearly the unhappy situation of the female in a male-supremacist society.

HE, SHE, AND IT

HE: So she, very imprudently, married the barber.

SHE: Very imprudently?

HE: That's what they say, of course. For a woman in her position, who had been accustomed all her life to every comfort, who was so particularly elegant and refined – whose tastes were so expensive, – to be suddenly reduced to twopence a year . . .

SHE: But she did it with her eyes open, didn't she?

HE: Oh, very much so. And that's what I can't understand. In all their remarks it's she who's to be pitied, who's to be prayed for, who's to be wept over, who's "thrown herself away". They go on as if he'd taken her in; but hasn't *she* taken *him* in just as much?

SHE: How can I possibly tell? I don't know the lady.

HE: But isn't marriage a free contract? If A likes to marry B, and B likes to marry A, what right has anyone to say that one of them is more responsible than the other for what happens afterwards?

SHE: You mean they put it all on to him?

HE: Exactly. They say "he'll have to justify himself"; which means, I suppose, that he'll have to make a considerably larger income than twopence a year.

SHE: Well, and won't he?

92

HE: I really can't see the obligation. She knows quite well she's given up her lace and her carriages; she's given them up deliberately; and why on earth he should be disgraced for ever if he doesn't get them back for her –

SHE: That of course would be ridiculous; and if they only mean that by their remarks I quite admit they're perfectly absurd.

HE: But what else *can* they mean? What do you mean yourself?

SHE: Something quite obvious. I should have thought that it's his business, and not hers, to support the family.

HE: Oh!

SHE: As for pretending that marriage is a free contract – but I suppose you're not serious. Of course it's understood when a man marries that he's got to look after his wife; it *is* a distinct obligation; and whether she runs the risk deliberately or not, if he doesn't do it, he *will* be disgraced for ever.

HE: Oh!

SHE: Of course you know all this, but I suppose you're leading up to something else. Only it does strike me as rather amusing that you should come here bursting with such righteous indignation at what after all is nothing more nor less than your own institution.

HE: Dear me! My own institution? I don't understand. You hurry one on so. Whatever I meant to lead up to, it certainly wasn't this. What have I instituted?

SHE: Everything! The whole thing's your doing. The whole arrangement of marriage, of society, of women. There's nothing in it that hasn't been carefully regulated by your commands, to suit your own convenience. You've tried by every means in your power to make it impossible for a woman to think by herself, or to act by herself; you have forbidden her to earn her own living; and now you complain because, when she marries, we think it right that her husband should earn it for her.

HE: I seem to be answerable for a great deal. I imagine it's because I'm a man; and I admit I had hoped that in conversations with you at any rate that fact might have been forgotten. I am always so eager to argue these matters from what the politicians call a strictly non-party standpoint. Couldn't you – it would make discussion so much easier – think of me for a minute or two as a woman?

SHE: It would be delightful. But if I do, wouldn't it be the right thing for *you* to imagine *me* to be a man?

HE: That will be rather risky, but I think we may take the risk; in the interests of truth, you know. And I shall begin at once by saying, as a woman to a man, that I deeply sympathize with the irritation you seem to feel towards the rest of your sex.

SHE: As a man, I am indeed astonished and annoyed at the perversity displayed by most of my fellow men whenever they open their mouths upon this topic. I once met a disgracefully fat banker who told me that *he* was ready to give women votes if *they* were ready to become policemen, or go into the army; and when I suggested that if that was the test he himself would certainly be disfranchised, he became exceedingly angry, and said that personal remarks were not arguments.

HE: Just what he would say, of course. And I'm afraid his wife would have agreed with him. I'm sorry to say that the majority of my sex too are quite as bad as the majority of yours. But don't for goodness' sake let's talk about them any more. They're really too stupid; and isn't it, after all, we ourselves who are the important people? Let's only talk about what we think ourselves. And to begin with, what *you* think.

SHE: My opinions are quite simple, but I suppose they're distinctly "advanced". I can't see what it is that should prevent you ladies from living very nearly exactly as we men do. There are physical differences of course, but I believe those are the only differences, and they don't seem to me to be very important. Suppose you were always treated exactly as men are treated, suppose you were educated as men are educated, suppose, if you like, you were dressed as men are dressed, wouldn't it be true that for nearly all intents and purposes you would be the same as men? I can't believe that your minds are radically different from ours, and that it isn't simply because we've always treated you in this perfectly ridiculous way that you appear to be flightier and stupider, and less logical than we. Just think of the difference in our education! From the nursery upwards were you ever supposed to be a rational human being at all? Were you ever trusted as your younger brother was trusted? Were you ever allowed to do what you liked half as much as your younger brother? Were you ever allowed to enjoy yourself half as much, or to get half as dirty as he? And have you ever in your whole life been allowed to be out by yourself after dark? Reflect on your younger brother's experiences, and reflect on your own! You know nothing – nothing but what you've picked up from novels, and from drawing-room conversations, and from what you've been told by other women as ignorant as yourself – of the real world, and real things, and real people. Your younger brother has led his company into battle by the time you are beginning to think of smoking your first cigarette; your younger brother has got drunk, and gambled, and done things that he oughtn't with various improper persons by the time that you are venturing in the privacy of your chamber to look into *Tom Jones*. When you're about fifty you will be knitting in a cap beside the fire, and your younger brother will be ruling twenty million blacks.

HE: My younger brother, I find, is a man of some distinction.

SHE: Yes. But not more distinguished than you. And that's what distresses me so much. You are so fearfully clever, in spite of all your disadvantages. If they were removed, wouldn't even your younger brother, perhaps, be put into the shade? Here you are, with your wonderful intelligence, your talents, your powers, positively thrown away on tea-making, and slipper-warming, and ordering the dinner! It's such abominable waste! Can't I see you as Chancellor of the Exchequer bringing in your magnificent budget? It's only with the weekly bills that you can be magnificent now.

HE: Your visions are charming, though they omit a good many interesting details. But I daresay those could be worked out quite well, and for the present I'm ready to let them pass. Indeed, it seems to me they *will* be worked out – sooner or later; things seem to be tending just in the direction you want them to tend in. I can quite conceive that in a few hundred years or so women will be practically men. I think that state of affairs will have all the advantages you give it; but there is one drawback which depresses me so much that it seems to wreck the whole thing. As a woman I protest against being turned into a man.

SHE: Why?

HE: Because I should have no one to be in love with, and there'ld be no one to be in love with me. Is it possible for a man to be in love with a man?

SHE: Really, need we go into that? I particularly excepted the physical part –

HE: But I'm not talking about the physical part. All I say is, if I'm to be Chancellor of the Exchequer, whose to fall in love with me? The First Lord of the Treasury? I never heard of such a thing.

SHE: I don't see why, if you were Chancellor of the Exchequer, and a woman, it mightn't happen. If you were a woman, what difference would it make whether you were Chancellor of the Exchequer or not?

HE: I believe it would make all the difference in the world. People do fall in love with minds as well as with bodies; you admit that? You admit that women's minds (for whatever reasons) *are* completely different from men's. My theory is that it's just this difference between women's minds and men's minds that makes them fall in love with each other. Remove that difference, by education or by whatever other means you choose, and what will be the result? Hardly any inducement at all for falling in love. Only, in fact, the physical one. And that, you admit, is rather unpleasant. Wouldn't it be rather unpleasant if the First Lord of the Treasury were in love with the Chancellor of the Exchequer in a purely physical way, merely because he couldn't be in love with her at all in any other?

SHE: If I were not a man, I think I should have to be shocked. Please be careful, and remember that I haven't been one long. It is very difficult to imagine such hypothetical cases, but I think on the whole I agree with you that it's improbable that any First Lord of the Treasury would ever fall in love with my Chancellor of the Exchequer. I grant you that; but on the other hand I don't agree that it's difference in mind that makes people fall in love.

You asked me whether a man could be in love with a man, and I didn't at the moment know what to answer. But as a man I must now say that I know such a thing is possible, for when I was yet a woman I had read Mr Jowett's translation of Plato. And if a man can be in love with a man, what becomes of your difference of minds? And, why should you object any longer to being turned from a woman into a man?

HE: You have said just what I wanted you to say. You have admitted that a man can be in love with a man. But I still think that this can only happen when the two minds are thoroughly different. In Greece boys were brought up and treated just as women are brought up and treated now; their minds were exactly like the minds of modern women. There was just the same contrast between their minds and the minds of men. It followed that men fell in love with them just as they fall in love with women now. So that it still remains true that this difference between minds is the great inducement to falling in love. But if you do away with the difference between women's minds and men's minds, you will put at once a vast number of persons whom it is possible to fall in love with out of circulation. And how are you going to fill up the gap?

SHE: You mean you'd fill it with boys?

HE: I think it would have to be filled in some such way. But that sounds very extraordinary, of course. At any rate it seems clear there'll have to be some new cross division, some utterly new conventional arrangement, for love. Will you admit that? Will you keep, though you become a woman again, an open mind? Will you be ready for what may seem remarkable developments? For men being in love with boys, for women with girls, perhaps? ...

SHE: Hush! I hear someone coming. I am a woman once more.

HE: But we agree?

SHE: We agree; and we are silent.

COMMENTARY
"THE PROPOSAL"

This delightful satire on the absurdities of the love-making habits of the upper middle class has the dimensions of a miniature portrait, and affords many of the same satisfactions. Strachey regarded the institution of marriage as an awesome thing; but the approach to it, as he shows in this story, is often hilarious. The manuscript bears no date.

THE PROPOSAL

His indecision suddenly left him, as he was saying Good-bye. It was all over now, he had done nothing, he could do nothing, and it was inevitable that it should be so. Yes, it was even simpler and better; for he could never explain what he felt, and perhaps nobody in the world would ever understand. As he turned away to go, and as he saw her sinking a little deeper into the deep chair, his mind turned too, automatically, towards outside things, towards the dog-cart, and his journey, and his catching the train. He took up his hand-bag and went towards the door, wondering indistinctly what she could be thinking of, and whether Oswald had understood about the pups. He turned the handle; and his mind completely changed. Resolutions are weakest when they are made up for ever, like those impregnable fortresses which fall by a *coup de main*. He could only think that he must be with her, that she was there, in the room, in the chair, behind him, and there was nothing to prevent him, and in a moment he was by her side. He was sitting upon the arm of her chair; he could look at her again; he knew again that infinite happiness. He did not even think of never leaving her; for he did not think of leaving her at all.

Was she a little embarrassed, looking down still, or a little angry? But what did it matter? For he was not embarrased, and he could speak now, easily. Oh, how much more easily than ever before!

"Has the Major sold his mare?"

It was his proposal; and, as he made it, he took her hand. She did not look up, she did not move. She said "I think he's gone into

Dalcott about it, with James." She had accepted him, and he knew it. The world shook a little, as he touched her hair.

"What an absurd looking man he is," he said.

"Rather like a frog," she answered, looking up at him and laughing.

He kissed her, gently, and said "You should see him when he hunts."

He slipped into the chair beside her, and embraced her. She said "Does he hunt much?" They kissed passionately, almost eternally; he was amazed. The clock's striking made him start up, exclaiming that he had missed his train. "There's another at twelve," she said. He looked towards the door, and saw that it was open; he must have left it so; and there was his bag, on the floor. He got up, and, walking across to the door, shut it, and put his bag upon the table. He walked on air; it was a pleasure to him to move his bag; he could not believe that what had happened had happened, and that, in a moment, he had discovered heaven. He looked, and saw that she was there. He ran to her, throwing himself down beside her, clasping her and kissing her, lost in the ecstasy of her embraces, the marvellous intimacy of her cheek, her neck, her breast.

"Redgie!" she murmured, twice, as he held her. But, for him, it was all silence; and for both it was all joy.

COMMENTARY
"DOES ABSENCE MAKE THE HEART GROW FONDER?"

This is the earliest Apostle's paper included in this collection. It was given on 19 November 1904, when Strachey was working on the dissertation on Warren Hastings which he vainly hoped would gain him a fellowship at Trinity.

Henry Sidgwick (1838–1900) taught moral science at Cambridge, where he was a fellow of Trinity. He had been the leader among his generation of Apostles as G. E. Moore was to be among a later generation, and his book *Methods of Ethics* (1874) had very great influence on Moore's own thinking. Sidgwick was greatly interested in the advancement of women's rights, and was involved in the founding of Newnham College for women at Cambridge.

DOES ABSENCE MAKE THE HEART
GROW FONDER?

As the Society has chosen this subject, I don't see why I shouldn't write about it. Whether the Society was exemplifying its accustomed wisdom when it made the choice, it is not for me to say; but at any rate there is a good deal of hope, for to begin to write a paper about X is quite a different thing from writing a paper about X. It is easy enough to bring the horses to the water, but to make them write a paper about X is exceedingly hard; they are always so anxious to write about A, B, C, and D instead.

I could continue for many pages these pleasant introductory remarks, but I reluctantly refrain. Only I cannot help noticing in passing that the truly good introductory remark is both apparently relevant and really relevant to the rest of the paper, but that it is not really relevant in the way in which it apparently is.

I wish to discuss marriage – but only the marriage of true minds, for that category includes I suppose more or less the Apostolic ones. Is it a fact that there are no impediments to their marriage? Allowing that it is possible that such a marriage should actually take place, allowing that the true minds exist in such circumstances as to make their marriage really attainable, can we proceed to say that then the conditions of true happiness have been secured, that there is nothing more to be done but to celebrate the nuptials, to consummate the union, and to leave the happy pair to themselves and their eternal affection?

I do not want to balance the advantages and disadvantages of marriage from the point of view of the Family or of the State; I wish to limit my inquiry to a consideration of its effect upon the minds of the two married persons. From this standpoint it appears to me that the disadvantages of marriage are overwhelming.

It is true, I believe, that the Scylla and Charybdis of marriage are boredom and lust; and I daresay that it is the former of these monsters who receives the greater share of the wreckage. Marriage necessarily implies that a large number of hours out of the twenty-four should be spent nose to nose; the strain of these perpetual privacies must become very great as time goes on; the two persons will almost certainly come to an agreement upon every point of any importance fairly soon in their married life; they will have none of those things to say to each other which made their former conversations so charming and so fresh; they will have to sink back upon these perennial interests of life – the wretched trivialities of the passing days – for the staple of their conversation; they will make jokes about Mr A's hat and Mr B's beard; and they will be bored to death. If they are not bored to death, there is I think only one decent alternative – that they should perpetually quarrel. The quarrelling married couple is a painful spectacle, but perhaps it is better than the bored one. The quarrels seem to be caused by the imperfections incident even to Apostolical human nature, which are liable to become intolerably emphasised during the intercourse of married life. Unfortunately it is much easier to perceive faults than to cease to have them, and it is almost impossible not to perceive the faults of one's husband or wife. There can be little doubt that this is particularly the case with persons of what Sidgwick would probably call a refined and sensitive temperament – the temperament, that is to say, which the best persons nowadays seem generally to have. It is only natural that when two such persons live together each should be constantly irritated by the other's conduct, and the irritation which they feel is particularly bad both because of the insignificance of the objects with which it is concerned, and because this very insignificance makes the irritation itself at once more difficult to express and to get rid of. The violent feeling of pent-up annoyance which is caused by the sight of one's husband or wife scratching their nose in a particular sort of way seems to me to be as degraded as it is common. A married life in which such feelings play a preponderating part can hardly be anything more than rather bad. But certainly by far the commonest condition in which married people spend their lives is neither one of active boredom nor of active irritation; it is rather the condition of the vegetable or the cow. This sort of middle state, where everything is neutral and uninteresting and tepid, is usually the haven into which the married couple retires after the exhaustion and failure of its earlier days. When this period arrives it indicates that the two persons have "settled down", that their emotions have left them – even their emotions of irritation and ennui – in fact that they are old. Such a state of mind, though it is certainly possessed of some sorts of mild obvious goods, appears to me to be one which every good person ought particularly to avoid; one is bound, I suppose, to reach it sooner or later; but let us put off the fatal moment for as long as possible. Is it not true that marriage is the high road leading straight towards this garden of Proserpine? The only hope of escape is to jump over a stile, and to pursue one's way along a footpath which is not broad enough for two.

These then seem to me to be the chief evils which the extreme proximity of two minds will probably produce – various forms of annoyance and irritation, and various forms of boredom and indifference; but there remain to be considered the evils likely to be produced by the extreme proximity of two bodies. The question as to whether the sexual emotions are or are not bad in themselves is immensely complicated by the great variety of such emotions. It is certain that they are sometimes bad; but they seem to be less bad in proportion as they lose the characteristics of what I am obliged to call, for want of a better term, pure lust. Pure lust is I think best seen in the case of self-abuse; nor can I imagine that the state of mind of a person abusing himself is other than very bad. But the characteristics which distinguishes this state of mind from other states of sexual feeling is that it is peculiarly devoid of fervent emotion, that it is on the contrary coldly deliberate, and that it is only exciting with the sort of excitement which is present in the scratching of an itching sore. The form of sexual emotion furthest from this – the most fervent, the least deliberate, the most exciting, – is undoubtedly to be found in the sort of love which is depicted in Romeo and Juliet; and surely it is true that the feelings of Romeo and Juliet are good in themselves, in spite of the fact that they are certainly sexual.

But the state of marriage is peculiarly calculated to annihilate the fervours of early love. There is the minimum of freshness, the minimum of inconvenience, the minimum of secrecy. Everything is arranged to make sexual intercourse easy and ordinary and dull; the *élan* which made the nuptials splendid must gradually come to recur at less and less frequent intervals, and at last altogether vanish; the embraces of a married pair must either dwindle into a mechanical contortion or be sullied year by year in a greater degree with the evil of pure lust. Even while ardours and excitements remain, constant proximity tends to produce evil in the lover's state of mind. The presence of the beloved object exaggerates desire, and the consciousness of this fact robs the feelings of the lover of their former spontaneity. He thinks about desire, he desires to desire; he becomes lascivious, and ceases to love.

It is clear that it is hardly possible for any of these bad feelings to arise in the minds of persons who love each other, but who are parted. In his absence, one naturally thinks of the best parts of one's friend; in his presence one inevitably thinks of his worst. In absence one is neither irritated nor bored nor inflamed by the remembrance of one's friend. One never wishes for him too little, nor too much. One's thoughts of him, though they may be fewer, are better and more truly affectionate. It is obvious, however, that two persons in absence can never attain to the heights of love. There can hardly be any passion between them; and letters are a cold substitute for kisses. On the whole I think the best conceivable arrangement would be one in which a short meeting took place at irregular intervals, between the two friends. This it seems to me would supply all the necessary conditions for a very good relationship: deep affection in absence, unmarred by personal weaknesses, by petty squabbles, by dreariness, by lust; and meetings and partings where the whole strength of love would find spontaneous and ardent expression. Mr and Mrs Z were obliged, I am told, to put these conditions into practice. Mr Z's health would not permit him to live in a cold climate; Mrs Z was obliged to reside among the snows; and they lived, the one at the bottom, and the other at the top, of a high mountain in Utopia. Once a year, however, – one never knew precisely when to expect the moment – the mildness of the climate allowed the two invalids to meet. Mr Z travelled half-way up, and Mrs Z travelled half-way down, the mountain; and they were usually able to remain for a day and a night in a chalet which was erected for that purpose. Happy Zs!

And yet – well, I cannot help confessing that if I had the chance of marrying in quite the ordinary way the person whom I wanted to, I wouldn't hesitate for a moment, in spite of this paper. Should I be absurd, and rash, and altogether wrong? I don't know. If the Society would tell me –.

Oh! I have not troubled to distinguish the marriage between the members of different sexes from that between members of the same. But I don't believe it was necessary, for, in spite of appearances, surely the difference is *not* fundamental?

COMMENTARY
"KING HEROD AND THE REV. MR MALTHUS"

This is another Dialogue of the Dead, an attempt at reviving that antique form that so interested Strachey. It has exquisitely funny moments, like the one when Malthus interprets the Massacre of the Innocents as a primitive means of population control. The purpose of this dialogue is also satirical, but it is of course the insufficiency of Malthusian reliance on self-restraint to control population growth that is being pointed up; in the end King Herod is the more rational of the interlocutors. But this piece does not have the bite of "Sennacherib and Rupert Brooke", for Strachey can hardly suggest that Malthus was as wicked as King Herod. At the very worst Malthus comes out of the dialogue looking like a rather doddering old parson.

The date of the piece is not ascertainable, but like the others in this genre it was probably written during or shortly after the war. It is the only work in which Strachey shows himself to be concerned with the problems of over-population and birth-control.

KING HEROD AND THE REV. MR MALTHUS

✿

THE REV. MR MALTHUS: I am delighted to meet your Majesty. I have always considered you a grossly misjudged monarch. You have my sincerest sympathy.

KING HEROD: I thank you. These are the first kind words that I have heard for eighteen hundred years.

THE REV. MR MALTHUS: No doubt your methods were a little violent – in fact, as a clergyman of the Church of England, I can by no means sanction them. But it is not your methods, it is your principles, that interest me and fill me with admiration. I hail in you the earliest exponent of the Theory of Population.

KING HEROD: You are referring, no doubt, to the so-called Massacre of the Innocents.

THE REV. MR MALTHUS: Quite so. And do not imagine for a moment that I am deluded by the ridiculous account which has reached us of your Majesty's motives in that affair. No, no; a reasonable man knows how to discuss the childish fantasies of ignorance and superstition. You were not a bloodthirsty tyrant of fairyland; you were a royal philosopher, who understood the great principle underlying the whole structure of the social fabric – the principle that population increases in a geometrical, and subsistence only in an arithmetical, ratio.

KING HEROD: I am appreciated at last!

THE REV. MR MALTHUS: You understood the fatal consequences of over-population – poverty, misery, disease, vice – an

108

inevitable decline in the whole standard of existence – and you resolved to prevent those evils at all hazards. Accordingly, you ordered that every child under the age of two in your dominions should be destroyed. The measure was drastic; yet it might well be argued that it was ultimately merciful, like the cruelty of a surgeon's knife. But the instincts of humanity were against you; your name has been branded with indelible infamy; and no other monarch, however enlightened, has ventured to follow your example.

KING HEROD: All that you say is true. I did not sufficiently take into consideration the profound irrationality of mankind. But you must admit that my position was a difficult one. I saw the evil; I saw the cure; and I was possessed of absolute power. Supposing you, Mr Malthus, had been King of Judæa, what would you have done?

THE REV. MR MALTHUS: As a clergyman of the Church of England, my position would have been so extremely anomalous that I hesitate to answer. But this I will say: I should have taken care not to outrage an instinct so deeply rooted in the human heart as the love of parents for their children. Persuasion is more effective than violence. There will be no need for a Massacre of the Innocents when you have induced men and women to realize the folly and the wickedness of bringing too many innocents into the world.

KING HEROD: You think you can induce them to realize that?

THE REV. MR MALTHUS: I am an optimist. I think I can.

KING HEROD: But even supposing you can – what then? My dear sir, I cannot help smiling. You talk of my outraging an instinct deeply rooted in the human heart; but what else, I should like to know, do *you* propose to do? What instinct is more deeply rooted than that which brings men and women together? And you quietly suggest that they should suppress that instinct – and you imagine that they will indeed suppress it, when once they can be made to realize that if they do not the world, at some future date, will be less prosperous! This is optimism indeed.

THE REV. MR MAZTHUS: Common sense and self-restraint is all I ask for.

KING HEROD: And that is much too much. A few stoical philosophers, a few fanatical ascetics, may follow you; but the mass of human beings will never set a limit to the begetting of children, for the simple reason that the begetting of children is the almost inevitable consequence of the greatest pleasure they know of.

THE REV. MR MALTHUS: Your argument is forcible, I confess. The almost inevitable consequence –! that is so indeed – would it were not so! And yet I remain an optimist. I cannot but hope that some way out of this dreadful difficulty may yet be found.

KING HEROD: Who knows but it may be? Mankind is irrational, but it is ingenious. I too shall continue to hope.

THE REV. MR MALTHUS: There are all sorts of possibilities; and I see no reason when they, at any rate, may not be safely left to fruitify – if I may use the expression – in the womb of time.

COMMENTARY
"ACCORDING TO FREUD"

This dialogue is another of Strachey's commentaries on the bourgeois war between the sexes. But the heroine is a rather startlingly modern liberated woman, who has read her Freud and has very advanced views on marriage. The piece has the informality – almost, one might say, the incoherence of a real conversation, and the observant reader might wonder if he does not catch a hint of Strachey's own voice in some of the odd inflections and curious turns of phrase. The author seems to mean the reader to reflect on the fact that the cause of misunderstanding in this dialogue is not so much what each of the characters says to the other, but what each of them assumes the other's presuppositions must be. The date of the piece must be 1914 – the year of the first appearance in English translation of Freud's *Psychopathology of Everyday Life* – or later.

ACCORDING TO FREUD

A country-house garden. On one side a large summer-house in the shape of a Greek temple with steps. On the other a seat. 6.30 p.m. on Sunday evening. Summer.

Enter Arthur, carrying a writing-block. He sits down on the seat, takes out a fountain pen, and begins to write. Rosamund appears in the door of the summer-house. Arthur looks up.

ROSAMUND: Oh dear! I'm interrupting. I'll go back to my book.

ARTHUR: No, please don't. It's only a letter. Do come and talk to me.

ROSAMUND: You're so polite. I daresay it's quite an important letter. And anyhow it's a very amusing book. I shall go and finish it, and leave you to –

ARTHUR [putting down his writing things and getting up]: No. It's a perfectly stupid letter, and I don't at all want to write it now. This is just the opportunity. – But I see what it is, you'd rather go on with your wretched book. – Polite indeed! – Very well, then, go along. [He sits down again.]

ROSAMUND: You've no idea how comfortable it is in there – a sofa with six gigantic cushions. Who ever heard of such things in a summer-house? – But it's very nice out here too. [She comes down the steps.] Just the opportunity? For what? [She sits.]

ARTHUR: For a little conversation, of course. Everybody seems to have disappeared – at last. Really, the publicity of the week-ends down here is appalling. After a day of it, one begins to feel as if one had been living for the last fourteen years at the Court of Versailles; and then in three minutes it'll all be over, and I shall be back again in London, and you – heaven knows where –

ROSAMUND: London too, very likely. But isn't your time-system rather incoherent? – Fourteen years? – Three minutes? – However, it really doesn't matter in the least, because you see, here we are – somehow or other; we're at the Court of Versailles no longer. How it comes about I can't imagine, but it has.

ARTHUR: Yes; it is very extraordinary. But these lucky accidents will sometimes happen.

ROSAMUND: Accidents? According to Freud, there are no such things.

ARTHUR: According to *who*?

ROSAMUND: According to Freud.

ARTHUR: I don't know the gentleman.

ROSAMUND: Of course not. You are wonderfully out of date. Who *have* you heard of? Schnitzler? Tchekhoff? I should like to put you through an examination in modern knowledge. Probably you've reached Ibsen, and are beginning to think that you really must take a look at this queer fellow Strindberg everyone's talking about – or was, the year before last. Well, well, I suppose in the end – ten years hence – you'll come and tell me that you've discovered a new writer, called Freud, who's very interesting, and you'll refuse to believe me when I answer, as I certainly shall, that I was reading him ten years ago, in that summer-house.

ARTHUR: I shall always believe anything of you. – So that was what you were reading? Freud: and what is Freud?

ROSAMUND: What is he? He's a doctor. But you'd better find out the rest for yourself, for no doubt you'll be shocked if I were to explain him to you. You'll find the book in there – on one of the six cushions. *The Psycho-Pathology of Everyday Life.* I'll leave you with it; and before dinner you will have learnt all about the impossibility of accidents, and the unconscious self, and the sexual symbolism of fountain-pens [she takes his up], and – but I see you're blushing already. [She puts it down again.]

ARTHUR: You bewilder me. One thing at a time. The impossibility of accidents first – the fountain-pen afterwards. When I forgot my handkerchief this morning, and had to go up and get one in the middle of breakfast – wasn't that an accident? Do explain. I'd much rather have it from you than the Doctor.

ROSAMUND: According to Freud, one never does forget.

ARTHUR: Oh, according to Freud –! But if I didn't forget my handkerchief, why on earth –?

ROSAMUND: I expect, according to Freud, your unconscious self left it behind on purpose, so that you might have an excuse for going upstairs and getting another look at the under-housemaid. You're blushing again. I think the Doctor's right.

ARTHUR: How ridiculous you are. As if –. But never mind the handkerchief. I'll tell you one thing. Your friend the Doctor *was* right about one particular accident – the accident we began by talking about – the accident of our meeting here. It wasn't an accident at all.

ROSAMUND: You don't say so!

ARTHUR: To tell you the truth, I heard you say you were going to read in the summer-house; and so I came here with those writing-things. It was all a fraud. I was going to burst in, and pretend to be surprised at finding you, and then –

ROSAMUND: And then?

ARTHUR: Why, and then, of course, we should be able to have a little conversation.

ROSAMUND: I see; it sounds very elaborate. But you didn't burst in; you sat down here, and began writing. Your story doesn't hang together at all.

ARTHUR: I admit that; I admit I sat down here. You see, when it came to the point, I thought I'd put it off. Don't laugh at me; I suddenly began to feel nervous.

ROSAMUND: Nervous! I can't understand a word you say.

First of all you eavesdrop behind corners, then you follow me about like a detective, then you decide to burst in upon me and pretend to be surprised, then you suddenly sit down on a seat, and feel nervous – nervous of *me*! – and all, apparently, because you want a little conversation. It seems to me quite inexplicable.

ARTHUR: You *are* laughing at me, you cruel creature. Rosamund, you know quite well what the explanation is. Or rather you know quite well that there's no explanation, that there never is, never can be, when a man's moved by his folly as I have been – by his folly or his wisdom, I don't know which – by some blind impulse or other that drives one about and makes one the prey of the most ridiculous hopes and still more ridiculous fears, and makes one hatch preposterous plots and imagine impossible scenes, and then suddenly plunges one into a realization of one's utter absurdity, and sits one down on a seat, pretending to write a letter with a – what does your friend call it? – a symbolic fountain-pen. – A little conversation! Yes, that's all I want – just a little – a very little. I'll be grateful for every drop. I'll wait patiently through fourteen years of Versailles for it, without a murmur, as you see. And then, when the opportunity comes at last, it'll certainly turn out that I shan't be in the least contented with anything so trifling, and shall insist on a great deal more.

ROSAMUND: Insist! Wait a minute. How much more, may I ask? you're so vague.

ARTHUR: I wish I could tell you. How can I define precisely infinity and eternity? – But this is all nonsense. – Rosamund –

ROSAMUND: No. Infinity and Eternity don't suit me at all. Big words like that make *me* a little nervous. What *do* you mean?

ARTHUR: Can't you see? I'm desperately in love with you. Isn't that enough?

ROSAMUND: Perhaps, if I could believe you –. But why should you expect me to do that? You know you *are* very polite – very polite and thoroughly out of date; I fancy you belong to the sixties. And in the sixties, I've no doubt it was the proper thing for gentlemen to make passionate protestations to ladies about Eternity and Infinity, and being desperately in love; but the ladies, in the sixties, were very well aware that that kind of thing was worth. And they had a very simple way of dealing with it. They referred the gentlemen to their fathers, and that either stopped them off altogether, or – but the difficulty is that *I*'m not in the sixties. I sometimes wish I was.

ARTHUR: Do you mean, that if you *had* been, you would have referred me to your father, like the rest of them?

ROSAMUND: Of course I should. Why not? It was such an obvious test. It was either one thing or the other, in the sixties. Either a man's intentions were honourable in the sixties, or else ... he had no intentions at all. I should have said to myself "Is this mere idle gallantry? Or is he proposing for my heart and hand?" And then I should have referred you to my father, and that would have settled it. But now –

ARTHUR: Yes, now, we're *not* in the sixties.

ROSAMUND: No, we're not. And for all the use he is to me, I might never have had a father at all.

ARTHUR: I understand you. My intentions – yes – quite so – I must confess I was under the impression – I had hopes – but – but I see I have gone too far.

ROSAMUND: You've been too polite, you mean.

ARTHUR: Perhaps; but it was unintentional. Rosamund, do *you* understand *me*? Idle gallantry, indeed! If you think that *that* is what I feel you're out of it altogether. It's quite true I didn't mention marriage; but somehow I imagined that marriage –

ROSAMUND: Marriage!

ARTHUR: Yes; I somehow imagined – it was very stupid of me –

ROSAMUND: Marriage! Ha, ha, ha! – Stop! You've said quite enough: you'll only make it worse by going on. Do you know what I advise you to do? – Finish your letter. [Rising.]

ARTHUR: Good heavens, I've offended you! I'm a wretched blundering fool. But don't go; forgive me. If I could explain myself, I think you would. My intentions, Rosamund, whatever you may think, were not dishonourable – really, really, they were not. [Rises too.]

ROSAMUND: Indeed? I'm very glad to hear it. But you've been altogether on the wrong tack. Good-bye. [Going.]

ARTHUR [turning away]: Ah! You don't care for me at all.

ROSAMUND [coming back]: What nonsense you keep talking! – With your absurd vocabulary from the sixties. But, as I've told you, *I* don't belong to the sixties; I belong to the present day. And now – and now, Arthur, I am going to prove it. [She sits.] Sit down, and listen to me. [He sits.]

ARTHUR: What do you mean?

ROSAMUND: I am going to prove that I belong to the present day – that I'm a contemporary of Dr Freud; because I'm simply going to tell you the truth. And the truth is, I am in love with you – very much in love with you indeed.

ARTHUR: Oh!

ROSAMUND: The truth is, our meeting here was even less of an accident than you supposed. Do you think I didn't intend you to come and find me here? Did you really imagine that my saying – so very much in your hearing – that I was going to read in the summer-house wasn't simply a hint? – If you hadn't come. ... But you did come. You're here. Well! Don't go! Stay! – Now, now I've explained myself. Yes; I'm in love with you – it's simply that.

ARTHUR: Thanks. But don't you think this is rather a poor joke! I assure you *I* have not been joking. I must have given a more hopelessly wrong impression even than I'd thought, for you to feel yourself justified in laughing at me like this. I think *you'd* better go back to your Dr Freud.

ROSAMUND: I see; you don't believe me. How ridiculous you are! But I might have expected it. You *would* take the plain truth for a joke. No doubt if I'd begun some silly rigmarole about the innocent joys of married life, you would have taken me seriously.

ARTHUR: Married life!

ROSAMUND: Yes, *that* you would have taken seriously. But when I simply say –

ARTHUR: Rosamund, it's no use. The truth is – I see it clearly now – we're incompatible. You really *had* better go back to your Freud, and I'll finish my letter. Good-bye. [He takes up his writing-block and rises.]

ROSAMUND: I quite agree. There's fifty years between us. Naturally we're incompatible.

ARTHUR: We shall meet at dinner – at the Court of Versailles. [Exit.]

ROSAMUND [alone]: Oh heavens, what stupidity! – Back to Freud? – I suppose so. [She gets up.] Oh! He's forgotten – [She picks up his fountain-pen, which he had left on the seat.]
[Re-enter Arthur.]

ARTHUR: I'm sorry. I find I'd forgotten –

ROSAMUND [holding out the pen]: Exactly. Forgotten?

ARTHUR: Yes. [He takes the pen.] Oh, you mean –

ROSAMUND: According to Freud, you know –

ARTHUR: One never does forget. And you believe that? – Well I must go. [Puts the pen in his pocket.] Do you think I came back here on purpose? What rubbish! Well, I must go. Good-bye. I must finish my letter. How could I have finished it without my pen? And, as I'd left my pen behind, I naturally – what else could I do? – Good-bye. – Rosamund, I can't stand this any longer. We, we're made for each other. We must – [embraces her].

ROSAMUND [freeing herself]: No, no, no. Nothing will induce me to marry you.

ARTHUR: Marry me? What! – Nothing will induce you –? – Oh! –

ROSAMUND: No, nothing – nothing on earth. Can't you understand that? How often am I to say it? Anything else you like; but I will *not* marry you.

ARTHUR: Anything else I like – but you will *not* – oh! ha, ha, ha, ha! –

ROSAMUND: Now he's hysterical. Old gentlemen in Thackeray

always do get hysterical when things go too far. I've shocked him into hysteria. In another minute he'll be in tears. Oh yes, it's shocking, disgraceful, incredible, isn't it? But there it is. A young lady actually having the shameless effrontery to say things like that to a man! – That she'll do anything else, but won't marry him! – And you thought I was a decent respectable girl, who would make a decent, respectable wife for you, and – oh how I loathe and despise you! I never want to speak to you again.

ARTHUR: One thing at a time – one thing at a time, I beg. Whether you speak to me or not, at any rate you don't want to marry me? – You're certain of that?

ROSAMUND: Certain? What else have I been telling you all this time – ever since we began this – this little conversation? How often do you want me to repeat it? Do you want to go on asking me to marry you through all eternity, and me to go on saying No till the crack of doom?

ARTHUR: Good heavens! I'm perfectly happy, and you're divine. [Goes towards her.]

ROSAMUND   [moving back]: I may be divine, but *you*'re out of your head, I think. After hysteria, lunacy.

ARTHUR: Very likely; the lunacy of too much happiness. But enough of this, my dear. You know quite well it was *you* who kept talking of marriage.

ROSAMUND: I?

ARTHUR: Yes, you. Was it your little joke?

ROSAMUND: My little joke? You *are* mad, I never said a word about marrying until you began.

ARTHUR: Oh, oh, oh! – And my intentions? And referring me to your father? And the joys of wedded life? – Oh, oh!

ROSAMUND: But – you maniac – that was in answer to *you* – that was explaining that I wouldn't – that nothing would induce me – that –

ARTHUR: Hush! You're the maniac. Rosamund, understand this at last: – I don't want to marry you any more than you want to marry me.

ROSAMUND: Arthur!

ARTHUR. My one object was to make it quite clear that that was what I *didn't* want. I kept saying so over and over again, and you took it for a proposal. It *was* a proposal, but you were so *entichée* in your notions of my out-of-date-ness that you simply couldn't believe I was saying what I was. It was a proposal ... of a different sort.

ROSAMUND: But – but – it's impossible; I can't have been such a fool. No, it was you who were *entiché*: you couldn't believe that I should take things simply; you thought I *was* in the sixties – if *you weren't*; and so you wrapt things round in such a mystery that you bamboozled me, and when I tried to answer, you bamboozled yourself as well. It seems to me the only wonder is that we're still talking.

ARTHUR: Thank goodness, we needn't talk much more. We both thoroughly disgraced ourselves; but luckily there's still time for repentance. Let us repent! – It was a narrow shave, though; we were only saved from utter ruin by –

ROSAMUND: By your fountain-pen.

ARTHUR: My ... my *symbolic* fountain-pen?

ROSAMUND: According to Freud.

ARTHUR: I'm beginning to think there may be rather more in Dr Freud than I'd supposed. I must read him. You said you had his book somewhere –? You must explain him to me.

ROSAMUND: Yes – in the summer-house. Come along. I'll explain as much as you like.

[They go into the summer-house.]

COMMENTARY
"THE REALLY INTERESTING QUESTION"

Social life in early twentieth-century Cambridge must have been very different from what it is in a present-day university, for the Apostles always met on a Saturday night. On 20 May 1911 Strachey delivered to the Society this paper, which is unusual in that it bears no title. The usual practise was to head one's paper with a cryptic question or phrase ending in a query; the other Apostles' papers included in this collection follow this convention. Another convention of the Society was a peculiar use of antiquated philosophical jargon; the Apostles were fond of referring to mundane matters as "phenomenal", reserving the opposite terms, "noumenal" and "real", for matters connected with the Society. Thus when Strachey in this essay speaks of the "phenomenal" world of newspapers, books, and women, he is contrasting it to the "real" world which consists of conversations among Apostles. Non-Apostles were often referred to, with some sense of irony, as "phenomena". This essay is not exceptional in its Apostle-centred concerns; it was quite normal for discussions to reflect the delight the members took in musing on themselves and their predecessors. The earlier generation of Apostles mentioned by Strachey had been especially distinguished, and it is with a sort of pride that Strachey reviles them for the artificiality and coldness of their behaviour to each other.

Frederick William Maitland (1850–1906) was Downing Professor of English Law at Cambridge. The biography mentioned in the text was published in 1910, and its author was the equally famous H. A. L. Fisher. Sir Frederick Pollock, Bt., KC (1845–1937) was another very distinguished jurist, who collaborated with Maitland on *The History of English Law before the Time of Edward I* (1895).

Arthur Woolgar Verrall (1851–1912) was a Fellow of Trinity. He was a Greek scholar, and one of the first of his discipline to treat the classics as works of art. Henry Jackson, OM (1839–1921) was Regius Professor of Greek, and also a Fellow of Trinity. Jackson was the great upholder of the traditions of the Society, and Strachey had to persuade him to relax the rule that no freshman might be elected to the Apostles, when he wanted to elect a young man with whom he had fallen in love. Strachey succeeded in securing the election of the freshman candidate, but his intellect was less distinguished than his looks, and his career as an Apostle could not be accounted a success. Bertrand Russell may have had this affair in mind when he remarked, in the first volume of his autobiography, that when Strachey was an Apostle "homosexual relations among the members were for a time common, but in my day they were unknown".

THE REALLY INTERESTING QUESTION

The really interesting question is always the particular one; but it's only the general one that it's possible to discuss. This sounds fatally like a quotation from last Saturday. But then one always does quote from last Saturday; one is hag-ridden by last Saturday; everything that could possibly be said on any subject was said last Saturday; the whole of life is nothing but last Saturday; and it will be last Saturday when one dies. Well, well, I face the fact, and proceed. The really interesting question is always the particular one; but it's only the general one that it's possible to discuss. The really interesting question concerns me – the particular me – and Alexis – the particular (but not *too* particular) Alexis. It concerns the particular kiss I gave him on a particular day, in the sun, with the hollyhocks all round, and the lawn, and some confused people out of sight in the distance – don't you see it all? Oh, but it's just the *all* that you don't see. For what do you know of a hundred infinitely important details – the precise curiosities of our relation, and whether it was before or after lunch, and the colour of the dear fellow's hair? And then – what amazements and glories! How the world changed in the twinkling of an eye – etc. etc. – I was going to write a poem about it – but who writes poems, now that Horn has come out, except on motor-buses and the very poor? – I admit it, I admit it, and have reduced myself to prose. – All that perhaps you might imagine. You might even imagine the singular sequel – the second kiss, inevitably so desired, and so inevitably bound to surpass even the wonders of the first – and then, just in that very moment, the disappointment, the failure, the ruin, and the dust – and Alexis, very dull, rather ugly, and almost bald, sitting beside me. All this can be imagined, and speculated on – the odd twist, and the curious mathematical difficulty, and the possibilities of such things – yes it's amusing, it's interesting; but what is there to discuss?

There is really only the general question to discuss; and there are two objections to doing so – (1) it was discussed – wasn't it? last Saturday, and (2) it's so very unpleasant. But neither of these objections seem to be of much weight. They were disregarded – weren't they? – last Saturday, and so they may as well be now. – Does the Society notice, by the by, how I *do* face facts? It's quite surprising.

In the meantime, I want the Society to reflect, not upon one kiss, nor two kisses, nor the strange impossible betwixt and between – but upon kisses in general – no, upon more than that – upon all those acts, from the bright smile to the most serious copulation, which give expression to the affections that we feel. It's curious how little these expressions – so immensely important and complicated and remarkable – have been considered by persons – writers and moralists – whose business it clearly is to do so. To judge from French novels, it's always a case of copulation or nothing; to judge from English novels, it's always a case of nothing. And then, the moralists – but they, poor dears, can hardly be expected to throw much light on such a subject. Who are they to decide such subtle questions as the propriety of groping or the principles of an embrace? That, of course, is the business of the Society. Otherwise all that we have to guide us are the dimmest and most conventional traditions – such as that, so long as one's in a conservatory, one may always kiss a woman, and, unless one's dying, after having won the battle of Trafalgar, one may never kiss a man.

But first, as to the facts. I have a vision of the world of persons in its ordinary intercourse as a plain with Gothic castles built upon it, far apart from one another, strongly fortified, with high walls and narrow windows and alarming moats. The inhabitants of one castle peer out from behind their fortifications, and from time to time catch sight of some dim motion in a neighbouring castle – some fluttering behind a rampart, or a hand from an arrow-slit waving a handkerchief, or a flag waving from a tower, or once a year or once a lifetime – an armed figure appearing on a parapet, with his vizor down. And that is all the castles ever get to know of each other. Is this an exaggeration? Not, surely, of the ordinary intercourse of ordinary people: and perhaps not of even – if one comes to consider things – of the extraordinary ones. If one comes to consider, isn't it rather singular, how little even the most expansive of us show what they feel? – I mean in comparison with what they *do* feel about other people. No doubt we all show something – and even that is important – in the small perpetual intercourse of daily life. But anything more than that –? Anything unusual or individual –? Once a year or once a lifetime, possibly; but otherwise with what a scrupulous, with what an almost bleak conventionality, we move! We might almost be business men, or members of the Cambridge Conversazione Society in the year 1880. Do I exaggerate? No doubt there are outbursts, no doubt there is a continual subtle something or other of intimacy – which makes a difference. But that only comes to the pulling down of a wall or two, and the widening of the windows; the dreadful castles themselves remain. How often I've peered out of mine! – After all, is there anything else to do – especially when one's castle happens to be built in King's Parade? – And how rarely and with what a strange excitement, have I seen the fluttering of a handkerchief or the hoisting of a flag! I can almost count the occasions. And then to think that those other castles I watch so eagerly have themselves perhaps – almost certainly – their excited enthusiastic inhabitants, bursting with wild curiosities and extraordinary communications – and all so silent there, so dark and mysterious, behind their walls.

That is what seems to me to be the state of things. I don't wish to suggest that it is wrong – only that it is queer. I see the advantages of the castle system – even at its most rigid. I even have a secret admiration for the typical Englishman – the strong silent man with the deep emotions – too deep – Oh! far too deep – ever to come to the surface; I can't help being impressed. And the disadvantages of expressing one's feelings are obvious enough. There is the uneasiness and the doubt which it may introduce into relationships; there is the possibility of the feelings expressed being in some way untrue; and there is that unfortunate complication of lust. The lust question seems very puzzling. Is it true that one is always, to some extent, in lust when one wants to express one's affections? I think so; but the really important question is – to *what* extent? The two things get so singularly mixed, and it needs a mind of steel to have the nerve to disentangle them. An apparent expression of affection which is a mask for lust appear to me to be undesirable among civilized human beings – it amounts to a breach of trust. But the difficulty is that, if all expressions of affection contain lust, the question as to whether any particular one is a *mask* for lust becomes, often enough, almost painfully subtle. It seems clear: at any rate, that those expressions in which affection *predominates* are best. Isn't it clear? Because really lust is such a distraction. Surely the *best* moment is the embrace before copulation – or after; copulation itself . . . is copulation. That is the extreme case; but it applies down all the degrees of expressions – even to looks. There is always, whenever one shows that one likes a person, a tendency towards that edge irrelevant business of lust. It is as if, by some preposterous dispensation of nature, one had to . . . . . . forth whenever one poked the fire. In such circumstances perhaps it would not be surprising that some people should prefer not to poke the fire more than once a day.

All this may be true, and yet – and yet . . . I had an experience lately. . . . For a month or two I lived in the same house with a woman, with whom I soon came to be on the most affectionate terms. And, in this case, we – and especially she – made no bones about expressing our feelings. Our kisses, our embraces – who shall remember them? No hesitations, no ambiguities, no botherings one way or the other over the sediment of lust; all was clear and direct and natural – affection flowing out just when and how it liked – the accepted, the obvious thing. And I wondered why all our affections shouldn't approximate in their expression to that type. Is it important that in my case the woman was only five years old? The human relation was there, and why should mere age make difference? What is there in knowledge and reflection and self-consciousness to distrust the current of our emotions, and make impossible the impulsive, spontaneous, exquisite expressions of our love?

I wonder the more because conventions seem to be slipping. With us, at any rate, the old rule of the curt Englishman, who feels (so he says) that his emotions are too sacred for him to dare to do anything but hint at them – that old rule has broken down. Even in my memory, there has been a change. Five years ago – the things that *didn't* happen! That's what, from the modern standpoint, strikes me now. And then – five years hence! – What a subject for a poem! – but no, we've given up poetry – we've reduced ourselves to prose.

To prose? A queer sort of prose, I think. But really, in this so-called universe, what else can one expect? To be sane, to be sensible, to view things from the ordinary standpoint of the educated man – I've tried that, and found it really rather painful. For a moment, under the pressure of *The Times* newspaper, of The Home Universities Library, of the Ladies, and the rest of the phenomenal world, I have succeeded in feeling sensible, and then, looking back on my previous reflections I have seen quite clearly that they were simply the crude and crazy vapourings of an eccentric in a dream. Perhaps that's why they are. So I think for a moment; but, opening the biography of our brother Maitland, I have a revulsion. Oh dear! the gay horror of those letters of our brothers Pollock, Verrall, and Jackson! The brave concealment of tragedy! The profound affection just showing, now and then, with such a delicacy, between the lines. – "I am sorry indeed that the part of your letter to which I looked so anxiously contained such bad news – and having said that I think that I won't say more – it is so useless." – "I feel good reason for hoping that before now you have become reasonably comfortable. What I wish you know." – "I do very earnestly hope that things go fairly well with you and that you have not much pain." – What a world, what a life, passing in these dimnesses! I see once more the bleak and barren plain, and the dreadful solitary castles, with their blinds drawn down.

COMMENTARY
"SHALL WE TAKE THE PLEDGE?"

This paper was delivered to the Society on 2 December 1905. Strachey had gone down from Cambridge. He was now living at home in London, incarcerated in the brooding hulk of 69 Lancaster Gate. The visit to Cambridge to read this paper was just one of the many visits he made during this year to old friends and old places in an attempt to escape the oppressiveness of the atmosphere at home.

When he refers, in the last paragraph of this essay, to "our brother Donne" Strachey is employing the Apostolic convention whereby the Society presumes to claim the credit for the eminence of certain great figures of the past by anachronistically attributing their genius to an Apostolic cast of mind. There is, however, a double joke here, for there was an Apostle named Donne (d. 1882) in the early days of the Society. In her book *The Cambridge "Apostles"* (1906), Mrs Frances Brookfield says:

> A scholar and a gentleman, William Bodham Donne was an "Apostle" of the earlier group and possessed all the fineness of aim and all the graver habits of thought which characterized that set, and to such an extent that he, after due consideration, left Cambridge without taking his degree, because he could not conscientiously subscribe to the formula of adherence to Established Church doctrines.

The "late Bishop of Gibraltar" was Henry Tomlinson (d. 1863), one of the founding members of the Society in the 1820s. The quotation from Donne is incomplete in the manuscript.

SHALL WE TAKE THE PLEDGE?

If I attempt to write about Love, I shall at least do so with a full sense of the difficulties of the subject. That Love is a thing that's too serious to be joked about, and too absurd to be taken seriously, that it's too hackneyed to say anything new about, and too perpetually new to be told the truth of – these things I know. I am besides aware that in the present case there is a circumstance which makes it peculiarly difficult for me to have anything of any value to say about Love. In spite of the hoariness of my age when it is compared with that of our youngest brother, the fact remains that in the eyes of the phenomenal world, of the angelic host, etc. I am young – almost ridiculously young. *Si jeunesse savait* – ! But how can it? My acquaintance among women is small; I know very few with anything approaching intimacy; and I must confess that I have never been in love with one. Brothers may therefore judge of the temerity with which I approach this paper, and of the sort of experience I possess upon the subject of it. I have, of course, fallen back upon my imagination, and upon that kind of second-hand experience which can be gathered through the agency of novels, and, on some rare occasions, of conversations. Someday I hope to be able to achieve the real thing. In the meantime I write papers about it for the Society.

My boldness is all the greater, because what I want to discuss is not concerned with the outworks and vague approaches, the opalescent penumbra, of Love, but with its most secret places, its most glowing centre, the blazing heart of the astounding citadel. I want to explore these innermost recesses, and, from the mystery of their depths, to bring back, imprisoned between my palms, some drops of the golden rain. Dear me! I seem to be already riding off on some high imaginary Pegasus: so wildly is my imagination stirred by these visionary ecstasies – visionary, I mean, to my youthful inexperience! How impatient I am – but after all, perhaps I should be contented. Is it not better to leave these penetralia unexplored? Ought we not to hold under strict control the natural impetuosity of our desires? This is the question I want the Society to answer for me. I am perpetually confronted, in my researches into the Philosophy of Loving, with two opposing doctrines which it appears to be impossible to reconcile or even to transcend. On the one hand, there is what may be called the ordinary Pagan point of view. It is the point of view which underlies nearly all amatory poetry, and which, I believe, dominates almost entirely the practical conduct of love. It seems to be the natural one: that which commands that we should, when we love, push our affection to the furthest to which it will go; that our love should traverse every limit; and that we should express its utmost fervours with our bodies no less than with our souls. It was this feeling that Romeo gave utterance to when he exclaimed "well, Juliet, I will lie with thee to-night". The other doctrine is of a completely contrary nature. It is that which Plato appears to put forward in the *Phaedrus*, and which underlies a great part of the ethics of traditional Christianity. According to this view, it is better to refrain than to achieve; the real triumph of the spirit takes place when the physical expression of love is held in restraint, so that the profoundest abysses of love's ocean remain for ever inviolate. The doctrine is a temperance doctrine; it would have us take the pledge. Of the arguments in favour of this latter view, those most generally urged are, I think, the least important. They are those which regard the question from the point of view of means. I do not wish to spend much time upon them, though doubtless they suggest some interesting matters for discussion. But, when I hear them used, I am often irritated because it seems to me that they are constantly brought forward as arguments to prove that temperance in love is good in itself. Thus I can imagine its being seriously stated that the condition of mind of two lovers copulating was bad because it would injure their health if they did so for more than a certain amount of time a day. This is an obvious absurdity, but very similar arguments are, I think, often used. It is stated that copulation is bad in itself because a feeling of revulsion sometimes takes place after it; or, because it may eventually become an obsession; or because it may cause a decrease in the affection between the lovers. All these considerations must, of course, be taken into account in any complete philosophy of love; but they are irrelevant when we are simply asking which state of mind is best in itself. It is to this question that I want brothers to give me an answer.

Personally, I must confess that there are many moments when I feel inclined to pin my faith to the flagstaff of Temperance. I find the idea of a superb restraint a wonderfully eminent one. But it is necessary to distinguish: the peculiarly Christian standpoint is never mine. The orthodox Christian ought, I think, to regard the extreme manifestations of love as bad in themselves because in the first place they show an exaggerated estimate of the value of earthly things as opposed to heavenly, and in the second place because these manifestations appear to him to be fundamentally indecent. Both these beliefs appear to me to be contained in the sort of Christian ascetic disapproval of violent love. Poor God may perhaps be dismissed without a word; and, as far as indecency goes, why, it may be asked, should the act of copulation be regarded as essentially different from every other function of the body? And really who nowadays would be so rash as to assert that farting and forthing – though they may be allowed to be fundamental – are fundamentally indecent?

The Platonic view, though mysterious, is certainly quite distinct from the Christian. It seems to be based upon two feelings – first, that any emotion becomes bad when carried beyond a certain point, and second, that that state of mind is a bad one in which the will is completely overmastered by passion. It is difficult not to have both these feelings very strongly when one reflects upon the matter. But ought we to have them? It is only natural that when we are cool we should admire coolness, that when we are collected we ought never to lose our heads. But why jump to the conclusion that we are more likely to be right when we are cool and collected than when we're excited and hot? And, when we're excited and hot, have we any very strong belief in the virtues of temperance?

The problem is a hard one, and it becomes the harder when we try to find out what our precise state of mind is – or (brothers must remember my inexperience) would be – during moments of unrestrained passion. From what I have been able to collect upon the subject, it seems certain that one's state may vary from one composed almost entirely of lust to one in which there is hardly any other feeling but that of intense affection. It is this latter state which, if it ever takes place, appears to me to be in reality better than the most exalted Platonism. I admit, indeed, that the mere slaking of desire – the performance of actions for the sake of physical pleasure alone – almost necessarily involves a bad state of mind. But my contention is that these very actions may become transmuted so completely as to lose their original nature. They may cease to be the expressions of bodily desire and become the expressions of affection. Nor do I believe that it is possible to reach the greatest heights of affection unless one has resort to these physical methods of expressing it. An existence without such heights appears to me a mediocre waste, ill recompensed by a frigid eminence. I don't mean to take the pledge.

Our brother Donne agrees with me. I quote from his greatest poem, "The Ecstasy", a passage which explains my theory more completely than I have been able to in this faint fizzle of a paper, shooting meteor-like between a phenomenal dinner and the eternities of true existence. But it is pleasant to be able to make the late Dean of St Paul's shake hands with the late Bishop of Gibraltar.

"But alas!" says the former, after describing the spiritual union of two lovers:

> [so long, so far
> Our bodies why do we forbear?
> They are ours, though they are not we. We are
> The intelligences, they the spheres.
> We owe them thanks, because they thus,
> Did us, to us, at first convey.]

PIECES FROM THE MARGIN
OF LITERATURE

COMMENTARY
"DIARY OF AN ATHENIAN, 400 BC"

Strachey had obviously been much impressed by reading the dialogues of Plato, mostly in the splendid, if reticent, Victorian translations of Benjamin Jowett. This rather too delicate story is the product of this reading. It is important for an understanding of Strachey's homosexuality, for it shows how he justified his sexual preference by what we might call the Greek Example. "Diary of an Athenian" seems rather juvenile; it appears to be a schoolboyish attempt to up-date Plato, and it contains rather too many allusions for the taste of anyone but the ambitious young writer who wants the reader to appreciate the breadth of the author's own reading. The manuscript is enigmatically dated "–? 1900 (?)", at which time Strachey was actually twenty years old.

The characters are taken from Platonic dialogues. Lysis is a character in the eponymous dialogue, which deals with the nature of friendship; Menexenus is there his "particular friend", but is the cousin of Ctesippus, another character in the dialogue, and not, as in Strachey's version, of Lysis, the son of Democrates. Glaucon, who appears to be the lover in Strachey's tale, is the son of Ariston and plays an important role in *The Republic*; Agathon, the narrator and the beloved of Glaucon, is to be found as the host of *The Symposium*, Plato's most important pronouncement on love. In that dialogue Agathon is a poet, and he makes a speech upon human love that satisfies everyone present at the drinking party except Socrates, who retorts to Agathon's speech with the lesson taught him by Diotima. The "bad horse" who holds sway over Glaucon refers to the myth of the two horses found in *Phaedrus*, Plato's extended conceit for describing the condition of a man when confronted by his beloved: the lover is like a charioteer whose chariot is drawn by two horses, one rational and benign, and the other wanton; each wishes to go in a different direction, and if the charioteer cannot get both to go in the direction urged by the rational horse, the chariot is in great danger of upsetting.

DIARY OF AN ATHENIAN, 400 BC

I sat this afternoon in the shrine to Pan built upon a spur of Lycabettus. Before me rose the hill of the Acropolis crowned by the shining piles of the Pantheon and the Erechtheum; on my left I could see Olympieum, the Stadium, and the Odeum; on my right the Agora, with its crowd of Stoa and Gymnasia, below me ran the silver thread of the Eridanus. I was alone; and the marble beneath my arm was warm from the rays of the summer sun: the trees of myrtle and of olive which covered the hillside shook lightly in the gentle breeze: upon my ears fell the shouts and the noise and the movement of the City of Athens.

There too shall I sit tomorrow, and many a time, perhaps again; but the Shrine of Pan that I left this evening I shall never return to in all my after life. To me it is no longer what it has been: a strange and holier light surrounds it in my mind; before, it was the abode of the god of nature; hereafter, it shall be sanctified besides by the god of Love.

The youths as they came out of the Palaestra laughed and talked in groups. Many walked away in the direction of the City; some lingered where they were; three came slowly forwards towards the hill where I was sitting. I recognized them all. The first was Lysis the son of Democrates; the second was Menexenus his cousin; and the third I knew too, and I was glad when I saw him coming, for it was for him that I was waiting in the shrine of Pan. They stopped at the foot of the slope, saying farewell. I could wait no longer, and leaning forward, cried "Well, am I to congratulate the victor? Or is he perhaps no victor after all? Lysis, has he won?" "Nay," said Lysis, "We'll leave him to answer that for himself, for Menexenus and I" – ah, Lysis! how gaily the words tripped over thy tongue! – "for Menexenus and I must be going." And he – Glaucon, I mean – and now you have his name, though I could not tell it at first, just for the pleasure of keeping it to tell afterwards – he looked up and smiled at me, and, as the other two ran off together, said "So you are there after all?" And I, leaning down over my balustrade, and smiling too, said "Yes, Glaucon."

III

Reader, – if reader there ever be of these words that I am writing now – and it may happen that in the years to come I myself shall look upon all this with a stranger's eyes – reader, pause here for a moment before you learn the rest. I desire not any to read further who reads not in charity and in knowledge; whose soul has not been purged with tears and fire. For I am glad as I write; and my gladness rushes out of me everywhere – from my eyes and my mouth and my hands – and what I write is what my gladness writes; and my gladness is my soul. Therefore there are many who cannot understand, and many who will not feel the joy that I feel, and to these I say "Do not enter here; this is no place for you"; but to others – to the few – to the two or one in all the world, I say "Read this if you list – it is yours by right – for you are pure and wise and will understand." Pure in the joy, and wise in the knowledge of Love.

IV

He came up the hill quickly, and sat down beside me on the marble seat that runs round the little platform in front of the shrine.

"So you think I didn't win?" he said.

"I?" I answered. "How could I think that? The Almighty, the invincible, Glaucon!"

"You think I didn't win?" he repeated.

"And your quails!" I said. "Your quails are magnificent!"

"You think I didn't win?" he said once more.

"What do I care," I replied, "whether you won or not? Your quail-fights are nothing to me. What interest should I take in them? What does it matter to me whether your bird or his kills the other? Besides it is barbarous and cruel – barbarous and cruel, I say – to set two wretched birds up to scratch each other's eyes out. I wonder how you can join in such practices – you, the most holy Glaucon. . . . But – but, tell me – did you win?"

"Little wretch!" he cried, "I shall pull your ears!"

"You had better not do that," I said, getting up, and looking out into the distance, where the sea lay in a pale strip upon the horizon.

"Yes, I did win," he said, getting up too, and putting his hand upon my shoulder. "I did win – this time."

"And if this time," I asked, "why not always?"

"Because," he answered, – "because it gets more difficult every time."

V

"My dear Glaucon" – I sat down again, and so did he – but we kept our faces still turned towards the view – "My dear Glaucon, you should talk to Socrates."

"Socrates?" he said, "the man with the ragged cloak?"

"Yes; he would tell you, most pious one, how to win your battles."

"But supposing I didn't want to win them?"

"He would tell you all the more."

"Supposing I was fighting with myself?"

"He would tell you not to let the bad horse run away with the chariot."

"Yes, yes, I have heard all that. But Agathon – Agathon – you don't know . . . the bad horse has the bit between his teeth."

"You should never have allowed that."

"Why not? Agathon, it's nature –"

"So is all evil."

– "And glorious" –

– "Not so glorious as temperance."
– "But what is life without it? Think of joy, Agathon!"
– "Think of virtue!"
"Delight!"
"Duty!"
"The poetry of Love!"
"The Honour of Life!"
"Sappho!"
"Penelope!"
"Necessity!"
"Restraint!"
"No!"
"Yes!" we laughed.

Then he stopped suddenly, and, laying his hand upon my arm "It's you," he said.

"Glaucon!" I said, with an assumption of surprise.

"Nay" – the words broke from him – "nay but I shall – I must!" And in a moment his arms were about me, and his breath was on my cheek. I felt like a hare in the clutch of an eagle, and yet I knew that I was safe.

"Let go!" I cried, and struggled from him, panting. Then I sat down again, with my back towards him, and my head buried in my arms. The thought of his sudden audacity held him motionless.

"You had better go away," I said.

"Yes," he answered. Then, coming nearer, "Agathon, I am sorry ..." I did not move. "Forgive me ..." I stayed quite still. "Agathon, I beseech you ... but I –" his voice trembled – "I love you Agathon ... Agathon ... and you care nothing for me?"

"Go away."

I heard his teeth clench as he turned, and went. Down the steps; then round to the left; then on; then – I looked out over the balcony and waited for him to come into sight; at present the laurel bushes hid him; but soon – soon – he would pass right underneath me – there. Now! "Glaucon!" I said ...

VI

The sun was sinking beneath the blue horizon, and the golden Athene on the Pantheon was gleaming red beneath its rays, as we two came out together from the Shrine of Pan, and walked down the slope towards the City, with our arms about each other's necks. That sadness which the evening alone brings with it hung upon the air – the evening which fills men's minds with thoughts of childhood by giving them a dread pre-knowledge of old age. A mist of grey and rose lingered above the town; and the whole earth was hushed and still and pale.

And thus it was that my joy became holier and more pure, and my heart, as it beat in my breast, was full of thoughts of Peace as well as of Love. A joy which cannot be told, a splendour and a glory past all imagination, buoyed me up upon their depths like a boat upon the ocean. It was perfect; it was complete. My soul was impregnated with the untold ecstasy, not as a sponge is filled with water, nor as a flaming coal with fire, but as a forest is filled with the tempest, and as the air is permeated with light. But in those last sad moments of the day I could not be overwhelmed: tears rose to my eyes; I saw through the mist the quiet fields of the country, and I knew that I had all – all that life could give; the battle was over, and its fruits must be enjoyed amid the sweetness of peace; I was content; I was content; ah! my love, your hand was upon my shoulder, your heart was upon my side!

VII

Stranger! Thus far you have come, and will you turn back now, that the first stage is over? Or will you rather proceed with me for your guide along that black road which lies beyond – into that dim land of the Future and which is unknown to both of us. You look askance at me; you like me not; perchance you think I am unclean. Stranger, you are a wise man; but let me tell you a story.

Erectheus was walking one night along the streets of Athens, when he beheld in front of him, with arm outstretched, the menacing figure of a Fury beckoning him to Hades. How clearly he saw the horrible whiteness of her countenance, and almost heard a laugh coming from her misshapen mouth! He stopped dead; then turned and ran, shrieking throughout all Athens that Erinys was pursuing him, in revenge for the murder of his grandmother. What think you then of this Erectheus to be thus startled by the moonlight shining on the Hermes in front of his

own house door? What devil had possessed him that he should
see this horror when there was naught but beauty for him to see? –
Nay it is simple enough, most noble stranger, – the fault lay in his
own eyes; – Erectheus was short-sighted.

I love because I love – not because it is right or wrong; and so,
I dare swear, do you. But while I love I believe and I feel and I
know that it is right; and so, I dare swear, do you. You know not
my love: what if I know not yours? You think of my love impure:
is yours so pure as that? Speak not of what you do not understand! To the pure all things are pure, and, though it is but
through the senses that we love at all, I say that my love is less
sensual than your love; and stand by what I say. Ah, stranger! be
not angry, and remember that the thing itself may not be bad,
though some make a bad use of it. Men call my love "the love of
boys". . . . I would rather name it "The Love of Souls".

COMMENTARY
"THE FRUIT OF THE TREE"

This short story is an accurate and entertaining verbal parody of Henry James, an author who fascinated Strachey greatly while he was an undergraduate. But the parody is only verbal: James's convoluted sentences are caught exactly, but Strachey has omitted to notice the other salient feature of James's writing, the complicated manner of narrating a story. Henry James has called attention to his own preference "for dealing with [his] subject-matter ... through the opportunity and the sensibility of some more or less detached, some not strictly involved, though thoroughly intelligent witness or reporter". But in "The Fruit of the Tree" there are no "reflectors" and no "reverberators"; Jamesian language is used, but Jamesian narrative techniques are eschewed in favour of a straightforward first-person narration. It is hardly surprising that Strachey failed to notice this factor in James's craftsmanship: there was barely time for reflection on the development of his narrative structures, as *The Awkward Age* had only been published two years before Strachey composed this piece in 1901.

If Strachey had been given to searching for explanations of the origins of homosexuality, the subject-matter of this story would have been another element in that explanation, for it is an English public-school romance. But Strachey never considered homosexuality a disease, and its etiology was never his concern. So in spite of its sombre atmosphere and hints of sado-masochistic feeling (an ingredient of the parody, perhaps), "The Fruit of the Tree" is really a celebration of the schoolboy crush.

THE FRUIT OF THE TREE

For you who understand there can (with one exception) be nothing in what follows there ought not to be. My story, if I have one (and in that very speculation there seems to lie so much of it) must, after all, be clarity itself to those for whom it is written, who are so exactly not those who would hesitate or boggle at a meaning. It's as right as anything – to you; and for the one exception to its rightness, which may be, precisely, my way of telling it, I must make, in advance, both an apology and an explanation. If I could only leave on you just the impression it left on me, oh! I should be thoroughly contented. It was deep; deeper, you know, a good deal than I was, or even am; so that, in the end, I found and perhaps still find myself swimming upon an ocean whose profundity it is altogether impossible to gauge. What he found – or whether he found anything at all – are questions which, though they add immensely to the complication – might perhaps eventually lead to a solution of the whole thing. At any rate it is certain that whatever interest my story has centres round just two persons, two characters, two phases. Its fascination is that it holds a perpetual antithesis between two such wonderful contraries. That one of them was he and one of them was I is really the least that can be said; there was (and I want to show it you) such a great deal more underneath. If I succeed you may have a glimpse of a conflict; the powers of good and the powers of evil you may see ranged as in the *Paradise Lost* upon the one hand and the other: if I show you that I shall be happy; what I shall never show you, and what, even more, I shall never show myself, is, in this clashing of opposites, exactly which was which.

I

I first saw him in something of a mist. Our eyes met among classrooms and ink, and when, in a moment, he had gone, mine only retained the general impression of a pleasant bigness, a radiance, a warmth, which, coming to me so soon after the cold plunge I had taken into the shivering strangeness of those new and bare surroundings, left me, if only for an unappreciable second, almost cold.

"Who's that?" I had flickered to my companion, who in his dirty collar was showing me round.

"That? That's Carlton," he said, and, when I, at his heels, ventured on a "What's he like?" I merely got for a reply, "A beast."

"I thought" – I took my courage in both hands – "he looked rather nice."

"Looked? He's not nice. He's –" he turned for a word – "you'll see."

Perhaps I rather hoped I wouldn't, and, whether I ever did or not, I decidedly regretted it when I thought I had begun to. He was, distinctly, a beast; his name, whispered in corridors, odiously preceded him; and, when he finally appeared, it was only in a dumb despair that one could possibly find refuge. But in those early days, which were bitterly summer, his presence, his existence, was, in my mind, only one small part of the horrid and general turmoil. He was, it is true, usually there, but so many other annoyances and perplexities were too that the addition of one more or less didn't seem to me so very much to matter. What did matter – oh, decidedly! – was the most disagreeable sum total. My agonized eyes, opening wider and wider every hour, at last failed altogether to take in anything at all but a universal dazzle of what was, precisely, not nice. At that period my view, there can be no doubt, was uncompromisingly, was violently, pessimistic. What was the good of calling any one particular a beast if everyone else in the place was just as much so? If Carlton, in one room, was obscene, somebody, in the next, would equally

144

annoy you by smacking your head, or by telling you to do something which you didn't, because of it, want to do. It was, so far as I could see, all dreadfully jangled, and it was only in time that I began to discern any differences, any regularity. When I did, though it added to the interest, it certainly didn't add to the pleasantness of things, to recognize that it was round the attracting figure of Carlton that everything else essentially revolved. He loomed, a fixed, mysterious, light through all that hazy and barbarous world. He was, I at last perceived it, the grand thing about it all, the thing, perhaps, that gave the rest of it whatever value, whatever interest, it might possess; and that I had grasped that was what made it to me so wonderfully absorbing when I came, with all the shock of inevitability, up against him.

"He's a beast" I, repeating in answer to a similar question exactly what, on the subject, I had been given to understand, had said to someone who, in spite of his obvious iniquity, naturally claimed by virtue of a common ignorance my confidence or even my sympathy. That this person had, in the hope of, as one termed it, "sucking up", gone straight to the subject of our conversation with a report of my remarks was, of course, only what might very well have been expected. After that there was a pause, and then, one morning, I found myself, suddenly, face to face with Carlton.

"I want to speak to you," he said, and I, recognizing at once that this was the first time he had expressed any such wish, felt very distinctly how unpleasant the interview was going to be.

I could only mutter "Oh!" and drop my books.

"You say, I believe, that I'm a beast," he menacingly continued, as I, quivering and helpless, shrank away from him. He didn't move: and, while I wondered what was coming next, I was able, fascinated, to take in his pose.

"I was told so," I hesitated; and then in a moment found him splendid and terrible towering above me.

"Am I?" he threw down at me.

"A beast?" I, looking up at him, quavered. "I – I don't know."

"Well," he magnificently replied, "*I* do. I am. D'you see?" and, after my feeble "Yes", went on. "You don't know me. You'll learn. I'll show you. I'll show you that I'm a beast. Remember that I'm a beast."

It hardly needed the concluding blow which I received full in the mouth to emphasize the physical violence of his words. I felt indeed, as if I had been hit all over, and when he added "That'll do. You may go", I obeyed, wretchedly slinking. During the next miserable hour, as I weltered dry-eyed through exercises and questions, the overwhelming impression of his bigness was, I think, what was chiefly with me. But when it was over, distressed, perplexed, infinitely hurt, and bitterly enraged, left alone at last in the bare and wooden schoolroom, I could, overcome by the strange vehemence of my emotions, only burst into tears.

II

Looking back on what, in those days, I must have been like, it is only with a difficult dimness that one discerns at all anything that isn't, in essentials, exactly not what might have been expected. That one sometimes can is precisely because it was just what I have to tell you that really made the whole enormous difference. The great gulf between the miraculous then and the no less miraculous now, is, to my mind, exactly spanned by the period of my story. That period, indeed, altered things so very ultimately that it is, as I have hinted, almost impossible to gather what, in actuality, occurred. That something did is – don't you see? – my opinion; and it is of this something, its steps, its movements, its landmarks, that I wish to make *you* the spectators.

What particularly strikes me about those few wonderful months is their vivid intenseness; they were white hot, they burnt, and, floating upon them, one betook, in some degree, of their incandescent qualities. If I was sublimely moral, Carlton was as magnificently unashamed. Between us, at least to my dazzled eyes, we struck sparks of inextinguishable fire. That this was in any degree possible, that I could in any way whatever find myself within the region of his high levels, was simply the outcome of the first twist of our relations. We were, indeed, coming together far quicker than anything else; but we approached each other with all the appearances of violent separation, which were, in fact, just the link which more and more connected us. It was he, of course, in the exorbitance of his power, who made it possible, while it was I, one must suppose, in the splendour of my isolation, who, for him, made it at all worth while. That I was

not averse to the process may be understood when I say that the
charm of it lay to me in, precisely, the view I was getting of him,
a view whose astounding interest grew wider and wider the
more I saw of it. When he let me flash at him "You're gloriously
vile" it only meant, after all, that I was beginning to appreciate
his amazing complexity, while he, as I conjecture, was really
wondering exactly how much further I'ld go.

Eventually we reached a stage which was, unfortunately, only
not the final one. We had a friend who, with his foolish propensi-
ties for unpleasant animals was as tedious to me as he was, to
Carlton, entertaining. He had been idiotic over a ferret, which, so
obviously male, Carlton had palmed off upon him as a downright
member of the opposite sex. He had taken the little animal with,
as Carlton delightedly exaggerated, "pills the size of my fist", and
now it was to inspect this doubtful acquisition that, in a dingy
barn, we came together. There, among the pigeons and the stoats,
the dirty straw and the still dirtier fluff, our eyes, behind the back
of our companion, began for the first time to intimately meet.
The squalor of the surroundings gave to our exchanges something
of a grand, an impenetrable, aloofness; our laughter, in its vivid
understanding, was as remote from the gurgle and the flapping of
the rusty birds as champagne is from ditch-water; our dull friend
as distant and dim as the Sahara. On our return our silence was
only the evidence of a mutual comprehension, and it was with
nothing of a shock that I heard him, putting out his hand, break
it.

"We'll, if you like, be friends." I did like very much, and
managed, putting my hand in his, to say so. That night, at tea,
we shared our jam and our sardines.

But I, at any rate, shared a good deal more than that. To be
constantly with him was, for one thing, a marvellous experience.
That I *was* immensely with him had for one of its results that we
were talked about, but one could sufficiently afford to ignore the
remarks of those who couldn't possibly have understood. Indeed,
caught up like Ganymede to the summit of Olympus, I looked
down with what was only scorn upon the wretches below me on
the common earth. They couldn't possibly understand, and I,
wrapt round through the warm winter with the folds of his
voluptuousness, had time gorgeously to muse of an infinite
series of seasons as delightful and as vast. But the future, with its

vagueness and its dangers, was after all, in my mind, only a splendid adjunct to what, of the present, was sublime. It was not only that in a moment my whole life had been wonderfully changed, transmuted, exalted, that I had gained, so suddenly, what in richness I had never imagined, dreamed; – I had found that which, unawares, I must once have strangely lost, mysteriously forgotten: I had searched, I had wandered, I had sighed, and now, in the fullness of time, I had achieved, I had miraculously attained.

III

His view, as you may have noticed, was, throughout, something of a mystery. Whether he had one at all was, of course, always a question, and, if he had, there still remained the further problem as to whether it was round me or round himself that his vision chiefly fell. If it was round me it would, decidedly, be splendid; but, much as I could wish it, I can hardly bring myself to the conclusion. He was so finely egotistical that any supposition of a centre, a pole, outside himself trembles very near the edge of the impossible. It is conceivable indeed that, for the moment, I became, for him, an amusing addition, an interesting new part, to his already immense personality; that is conceivable, but what is not is that, in his vast and sweeping range, he ever regarded me exactly as I regarded him.

One could, in fact, never look at him but with a sort of awe. One watched him as one watched a procession, in the admiration of silence; and the idea of a check, a failure, in that inscrutable advance came to one's mind as a monstrous, a shameful impossibility. He was perpetually magnificent, eternally superb; he soared. I, as I came upon him, found him like a mine, inexhaustible and glittering, before me, and felt, as I plunged deeper and deeper into his gorgeous recesses, all the joys of an intimate and unending discovery. We were, indeed, by our opposites, amazingly matched. Our conversations, like fugues, sparkled on heights, or descended darkling into the obscure recesses of absolute understanding. Through it all I exquisitely knew that he was mine to touch, to hold, to admire.

His confidences, his reminiscences, were supreme. He told me how, in his wild American days, he had, a boy among boys, organized into parties his companions who, scampering on ponies and stripped to the waist, had fought each other thus with whips and laughter. "It must have hurt," I admiringly ejaculated. "Oh, it stung. But," he smiled, "one always lammed them a good deal harder than they lammed one."

"You mean –"

"It was worth it."

"You're glorious," I could only exclaim, to which he wonderfully answered "I thought you thought the opposite."

That I perhaps did I was, later, to grasp. As the first flush of it began to wear off I distinctly again detected the old drawbacks, the old crudities. However much I liked him, what he liked was a different matter, and he liked a great deal that I, at the time, found it more and more difficult to swallow. I was, among other things, so devout a Christian that his splendid barbarism, his careless cruelty, often shocked and sometimes disgusted me. That I, at first, did not personally feel it made me, perhaps, a little forget, and lulled me into a dangerous security; but in time he deliciously began to discover that, after all, *I* was the handiest, and the most amusing, thing to torment. When we both saw it, it necessarily and violently hurried us apart. It was in vain that I threw imploring hands across a chasm which continually widened precisely because I didn't want it to. At last the final incident was inevitably reached; it was inevitable because, just in proportion to my quavering, he quite unimpededly advanced, and it was because of his advance that I quavered. The situation was therefore, viciously, a circle, which, directly its ends met, simply exploded. This occurred when, with a hammer, he plucked down the printed daubs which I, in my artistic fervour, had nailed to the walls.

"You're not to do that," I had furiously said.

"I shall."

"They're mine; I don't see why you should."

"I shall do just as I like to anything of yours," he disdainfully let fall.

"You won't," I desperately answered, "not to me."

"Yes, dear, to you," he replied, and, with his hand, made an attempt which was altogether indescribable. The acuteness of the crisis was only equalled by my appreciation of it. I felt, I could almost hear, my ruined past tumbling about my head. That I never hesitated for a moment seems to me now a wonderful proof of my detachment. I madly, with the blood in my face, seized the hammer, and beat, vainly, agonizedly, upon his immovable body. In a second I was overcome, held, tortured.

"You fool," he said, as huge, impervious, absolute, he towered tremendous above me.

"You don't care," it was my last appeal, "what happens to me."

"Why should I?" He unanswerably answered.

"You don't care," I wailed. He turned to go, and "I hate you!" I flashed at him.

"Why?" he pistolled, and, taking me by the throat, shook me.

I managed to splutter "Because you're a beast!" Then, throwing me away from him, he soared to a height which I, at least, before or since, have seen no other human being reach.

"You know quite well, young boy," was his astounding statement, "that *that* is not the reason!"

"Then what is?" I had just breath enough to gasp.

But, to my question, from his lips at any rate, I never received an answer. He vanished; and for me, through the dreary weeks that followed, trudging neglected in dirty and familiar roads, or loitering listlessly among endless cricket, remained the perpetual problem, the undeviating search. That I had lost him for ever was the groundwork, the basis, of all my speculations. He had gone.

COMMENTARY
"CURIOUS MANUSCRIPT"

This fragment of a story shows Strachey the homosexual apologist at his most militant. There is no indication of its date of composition: but the obvious parallels in the story with the plight of Oscar Wilde argue that it is an early work, written perhaps not long after Wilde's 1895 trial. Though Strachey and his friends have left very little explicit comment on the Wilde case, it must have had at least as great an effect on their ideas about sexual behaviour as did the Dreyfus case on their ideas about political behaviour. In both cases, as Leonard Woolf shows in his remarks upon the Dreyfus affair in his autobiography, the effect was to lead to greater militancy.

The law respecting homosexual behaviour was as confused as its application was wicked. It was only in 1885, when Strachey was five years old, that Henry Labouchere tacked on to the Criminal Law Amendment Act his own notorious amendment which made "an act of gross indecency" between male adults, whether in private or in public, and not amounting to buggery, an offence punishable by a maximum of two years' imprisonment with hard labour. It was this statute, whose promulgation was almost an after-thought, under which Wilde was convicted. Strachey regarded it as yet another evidence of Victorian hypocrisy, and would have rejoiced at its repeal in 1967. "Curious Manuscript, discovered in Morocco, and now printed for the first time", breaks off in mid-sentence just as the narrator is launching into an impassioned denunciation of the irrational laws governing sexual practices – laws that are transparently those of England, and not of the unnamed Islamic state from which the hero has fled. Indeed, the attempt to set the story in a Muslim land is a failure, as the narrator is only too obviously an Englishman, who, like Wilde, has been persecuted, estranged from wife and children, degraded, and forced into exile. Strachey's constant harping, in the last paragraph, on a matter of "eight inches" reveals a curious conception of female anatomy.

CURIOUS MANUSCRIPT
discovered in Morocco,
and now printed for the first time

This is certainly not a pleasant country, and you may perhaps wonder why I choose to reside in it. The barbarity of its inhabitants has pained and astonished me; yet I remain. They have maltreated me in the most distressing manner; but I am still here. They have descended upon me, they have carried off my wife, they have cut the throats of my unfortunate children, and I daily tremble for my own existence; why have I not departed long ago? why did I ever leave my native country? what is it that induces me to eke out my existence among deserts and siroccos, in company with savages unacquainted with the classics, whose sanitary arrangements are out of date, and whose chief form of amusement is to roast their enemies in front of the kitchen fire? It seems extraordinary that I should be here; but the reasons which brought me here seem more extraordinary still. Yet to you they may appear to be perfectly satisfactory, and perhaps it is only I who am struck by an absurdity which does not, in reality, exist. It is quite true that I kissed someone; it is quite true that I said I saw no harm in kissing anyone, so long as their breath was not unpleasant and they had no objection to being kissed; and it is quite true that I wrote a few words upon some pieces of paper intended for the sight of no one upon earth except myself. But are these, I wish to know, sufficient reasons for such an exile? It may seem to you obvious that they are; you may think it clear that I have committed abominable crimes deserving of disgrace, of ruin, of imprisonment, of solitary confinement, of the treatment which is reserved for forgers and pickpockets, and of the certainty of a miserable death. It is possible, it is even probable, that these are your opinions. But why are they your opinions, and the opinions of everybody else?

I am sorry to trouble you with such a question, but you will admit that to me at any rate it is of some interest in my present remarkable situation. Why am I in this situation? I am puzzled; I have to confess I have no solution to offer; and for a man to be unable to tell why the devil he is where he is seems, to say the least of it, a little queer. I little thought when I went to the University that I was laying the foundation for such a ridiculous dilemma. I should probably have omitted to enter that venerable institution, if I had known that I was dooming my last years to a concatenation of perplexities most unsuitable to a man of dignity, position, and some pretensions to taste.

If you can tolerate my story, it is this. – At the University I made the acquaintance of a young man, who soon became my dearest friend. We were of the same age; and our pursuits and capacities were just different enough to be pleasing, and similar enough to make our intercourse the happiest that can be conceived. For three years I loved my friend more than I had ever loved anyone before. Was this scandalous? Was this wicked? I ask, was this deserving of the severest punishment? I have no doubt that it was. But why? You smile, you frown, and you refuse to answer.

My happiness was cut short by my friend's death. He died in my arms; I fainted, I recovered, I burst into floods of tears, I bitterly lamented that it was not I who was dead. I was so unwise, so perverse, so despicable, and so utterly devoid of shame, as to write some poems in memory of my friend, with which I solaced myself in private, I was actually so abominable as to imagine when I read them that his spirit was hovering round me, and quieting my despair. Sometime afterwards I married, and settled in the country with my wife and family; for a few years I enjoyed myself as much as anyone could who had such a past to look back upon; but I was not destined to remain long in peace.

At the University I had made an enemy as well as a friend. This person had begun by hating me because I said what I thought, and did what I liked, and was not a Mahommedan; and he had ended by hating me because he hated me. I had forgotten this person, until one day I found out that he had not forgotten me. I discovered that he was taking the trouble to spread malignant reports about me, in order to undermine my reputation and destroy my position in the world. I thought at first that I could ignore such malevolence, and that no human being would believe what it pleased this person to declare was true. But I found I was mistaken; I was looked at in a way I had never been looked at before; I was asked extraordinary questions; I was suddenly left alone. I supported myself by writing, and I found it more and more difficult to obtain a market for what I wrote. This person was at the bottom of my distresses, and his insufferable stories were the cause of a financial loss which was increasing day by day. I was certain that at any rate a court of justice would expose his falsehoods; I sued him for slander; but I found that I was mistaken again.

I have no doubt that I was right to call this person malignant, but will it surprise you to hear that I doubt very much whether he ever actually did tell a lie about me, and I have never been able to discover why it was that his malignant statements produced any effect at all? That I prosecuted this person for a slander which I could not conceive to be slanderous you will own is an amusing fact; and that the result of my action is that I am now being hunted for my life by a hoard of brigands in the mountains of Morocco, you will recognize to be very funny indeed.

I agree that it is certain that this personage accused me of committing immoral acts with my friend; but I perpetually wonder what an immoral act is. Is it an immoral act to look at someone else? Is it an immoral act to touch someone else? Is it an immoral act to kiss someone else? All these are very interesting questions. It is also very interesting to consider whether it is immoral to embrace, whether it is immoral to make a seminal discharge, and whether it is immoral to copulate in a somewhat unusual manner. Supposing I had committed every one of these acts, are you quite sure that you are right to bundle me off to Morocco? Why, I wish to know, is it perfectly moral for me to copulate with a personage whose sexual organs are different from my own, and perfectly immoral for me to copulate with a personage whose sexual organs are not different? The point of penetration, you will remark, is not the same in the two cases. I agree; but is it entirely reasonable that a matter of about eight inches one way or the other should have such an extraordinary effect upon your judgement? Do you really never wish to see me again because a certain part of my body penetrated A's about eight inches from the point where, if it had been B's, it might have penetrated with absolute impunity? Are eight inches to send me into solitude for two years, or into exile for ever? I am ready to believe that it is just that they should; but you will forgive me if I express my astonishment at . . .

COMMENTARY
"AN ARABIAN NIGHT"

This Eastern romance set in a Scheherazade frame is whimsical and mannered, but pleasant in the same way that many of the original tales of Scheherazade are. Many of Strachey's stories are set against an exotic background, not simply for the sake of colour and romance, but, as in the case of this story, so that the author could construct a locale and a society where the prejudices of his own society could be suspended. Thus in the Persia of this tale homosexuality is not remotely regarded as anything but normal. Light-hearted as this piece is – it was certainly not intended to be anything but entertaining, and there is no reason to attribute any didactic purpose to it – there is a certain literary vision of Utopia implied in its assumption that homosexual love is to be talked about and acted upon as openly as heterosexual love.

No date is indicated for the composition of this story, but late in his short life Strachey acquired a serenity about his own homosexuality that fits the atmosphere of this story. He began to insist that while homosexuality might be statistically abnormal, in that it was not practised by the average man, there was no other sense at all in which it could be said to be abnormal, and certainly none in which it was "unhealthy". Though he discovered Freud rather early, and though his brother and sister-in-law were practising as psycho-analysts, he had nothing but contempt for the misguided members of that profession who felt that homosexuality was a "disease" that could be "cured". In a very funny letter to Carrington, written from Garsington on 3 June 1923, he speaks of a German doctor who had "treated" a young man of his acquaintance:

> After 4 months and an expenditure of £200, he found he could just bear the thought of going to bed with a woman. No more. Several other wretched undergraduates have been through the same "treatment". They walk about haggard on the lawn, wondering whether they could bear the thought of a woman's private parts . . .

AN ARABIAN NIGHT

There once reigned in Ispahan a great and cruel King; and one day, as he was riding near the City, he saw a shepherd youth, and fell in love with him. But the shepherd youth cared not for the King, and though the King sent him a letter of love, he replied with nothing but humble courtesies. Then, the King's desire growing, he sent a message to the youth with gifts of fruit from his royal garden and a wine from his royal cellars; and the youth thanked the messenger, but tasted not the fruit, nor drank of the wine, continued still with his shepherd's fare of goat's milk and porridge. Then the King sent another messenger with yet richer gifts of silk and of gold – golden ornaments for the youth's arms, precious pearls for his ears, and fine raiment for his body, and a silken turban for his head. And the youth thanked the messenger, but touched none of the gifts, and still went about his work in his poor shepherd's apparel. Then the King sent yet another messenger, and this messenger took with him three of the King's favourite concubines, dressed in silver and purple, and scented with cassia and nard, and brought them to the youth. And the youth thanked the messenger once again, but he turned his back upon the King's concubines. Now it happened that the blacksmith of the village was a handsome man, and his sinewy limbs and brawny body pleased the youth and filled him with desire, so that in the evening of that day he went in unto the blacksmith, and lay with him in an inner chamber. And the blacksmith's wife, looking through the curtains of the chamber, saw her husband in the arms of the youth; and she was jealous, and in her anger went to the King's messenger, who had not yet departed from the village, and told him what she had seen. And when the messenger returned to the palace, he told the King what he had learnt from the blacksmith's wife. And the King waxed wroth, and cried "What! Shall I be scorned thus by a shepherd's boy? Go once again to the village, but this time go with a rope and swords. And let the youth be seized, and his hands tied behind his back, and let him be brought before me."

So the youth was brought into the presence of the King, as he sat upon his royal throne, in his robes of state, with his jewelled turban upon his head, and his captains and his counsellors around him. Then the King bade them all depart, so that he was left alone with the youth. And as he looked upon the youth, his heart burned within him with love and fury. For the youth was beautiful to behold, dressed in his ragged shepherd's suit, with his curls ruffled on his forehead, and his hands tied behind him. And moreover he looked as harmless as he was beautiful. And the King thought "Is it possible that such a poor pretty helpless child should defy me, the King? No, surely, it is not possible." And then he thought of the concubines and the blacksmith, and the blood rushed to his head, and starting up from his throne he shouted "Ungracious boy! What hast thou done? How hast thou treated me? Dost thou forget that I am the King?" And the youth replied "Oh, my lord, who is your servant that he should not remember it?" And the King said "Thy words are the words of humility, but thy deeds are the deeds of pride. What favours have I not shown thee? What gifts have I not showered upon thee? – Wine, and gold, and gems, and fine raiment, and three of my favourite concubines scented with cassia and nard! Have I not stretched forth my royal might for thy sake? Have I not been as a Providence to thee? Nay, could Allah himself have done more for thee, than I, the King?" And the youth said "Great is the power of the King." And the King said "Great indeed is the power of the King, as thou, proud youth, mayst find to thy cost. For thou hast used me despitefully, thou hast scorned my gifts and turned away from my friendship – thou a miserable wisp of a Shepherd's lad. Why, therefore, should *I* now not use *thee* despitefully, in my turn? Am I not the King? Tell me! Why should I not kill thee? Nay, is not killing too good for thee? Why should I not have thee torn in pieces by my wild horses, or thy limbs broken on my chariot wheel, and scattered over the

City?" And he towered over the youth in his fury, and the youth stood as one amazed; and the King took hold of the youth, and shook him; and then the youth said once more "Great is the power of the King." And the King, turning away strode about the chamber, saying "Wretched youth, if the power of the King is great, then tempt not the King's anger!" And he stood again before the youth, and said "I have it in my heart to forgive thee. Speak! Think upon my favours, and say if in *thy* heart thou feelest not towards me a little love." "Does my lord desire me indeed to speak with my heart, or with my lips only?" And the King said "Thy lips? What care I for thy lips? Be careful, or I shall cut them off with my own hands!" And he fingered his dagger as he spoke; and then he cried "Speak with thy heart, thou foolish youth! And yet, what care I for thy heart? Be careful, or I shall have it torn from out thy body before my eyes! And yet, verily, speak with thy heart, oh youth, or speak not at all." And the youth said "Does not my lord see? How can the beast speak when the hands are tied?" And the King said, "What! Art thou insolent still? Dost thou think to play with me for ever? Surely it is time that thy indifference should cease. Thou Knave! I shall cure thee yet of thy coldness." And he gnashed his teeth, and stamped his foot, and called for the Captain of the Guard. And when the Captain of the Guard was come, the King said "What is the punishment ordained for contemness of Majesty?" And the Captain of the Guard answered "They are beaten with rods, and nailed hand and foot in the pillory in the market-place, and their heads are cut off, and their bodies thrown to the dogs." And the King said "Let justice be executed upon this slave." And the guards seized the youth and carried him away. But the King covered his face with his hands, and rushing into a private chamber, flung himself down upon a couch.

Now it so fell out that, as the youth was being led by the soldiers through the court of the palace, the Princess Fatima, the King's sister, looked out from her lattice, and her eyes fell upon him. And she was amazed by the youth's beauty, and sorrowed that one so fair should be so unfortunate. And she called an eunuch and said, "Go, I prithee, and ask one of the soldiers in the court, why it is that the youth is being led away, as it were to execution." So the eunuch went, and asked one of the soldiers, who told him that the youth was to die by the King's command. And when the

Princess heard this, she was overcome by pity for the youth, and cried "Oh, that so comely a youth should suffer so!" And then she took courage, and, going to the King's private chamber, she went in and stood before him.

And when the King was aware of the presence of the Princess, he looked up from his couch in silence. And the Princess said "Oh my brother, I see tears upon thy countenance." And the King said "Mistake not, my sister, they are tears of rage." And she said "And why is my brother angry?" And the King said "Because of a certain youth, whose name be for ever accursed." And she said "A certain youth, oh my brother?" And thereupon the King told her all that had happened since he had first seen the youth in the outskirts of the City: how he had loved the youth, and how the youth had used him despitefully, and of his gifts, and of the concubines and the blacksmith, and how the youth in his presence had spoken no word of repentance, and how at last he had ordered the youth to receive the punishment ordained for contemness of Majesty. And when he had finished, the Princess was silent. And the King said "My sister, have I not done well?" And the Princess said "Brother, assuredly thou hast not done well. Thou hast done foolishly. Truly the youth has used thee cruelly, but what will it profit thee to use him cruelly in thy turn? By Allah, what will it profit thee?" And the King said "Thou speakest wisely, oh my sister. But what wouldst thou have me do?" And the Princess said "Do as I advise thee, and thou mayst yet have thy desire."

And the King did as the Princess advised him, and he sent for the Captain of the Guard, and gave him commandments; and then he sent for the Chamberlain and said "Tomorrow morning, when the Captains and the Counsellors assemble in the outer room, draw not the curtains of my bedchamber until the third hour after the dawn." And then he ordered that he should be left alone; and when he was alone he took off his robes of state and his jewelled turban, and wrapt a cloth about his loins, and put a cloak upon his shoulders, and bandaged his head and his face with bandages, as if he had been wounded. And then he went out of the palace by a secret way.

And meanwhile the youth had been taken to prison, and lay there miserable. And towards evening the gaoler came, and the youth said "Is it now the time of my punishment, when shall I be beaten with rods, and nailed hand and foot in the pillory in the market-place, and my head cut off, and my body thrown to the dogs? Prithee, let it be soon." And the gaoler replied "Patience, good youth; *tout vient à point à qui sait attendre*", for he was a learned gaoler and had travelled in far countries. But the youth said "Gaoler, I understand thee not, but I think thou mockest me." And the gaoler said "*Chi lo sa?* But now, good youth, prepare for a companion in misfortune. For a certain notable brigand has been captured in the mountains, and has been brought to the prison, and he is to spend the night with thee." And as he spoke, the door opened, and the guards pushed in the King in his cloak and his bandages, as if he were the captured brigand; and he and the youth were alone together.

And they talked together, and grew friendly; and the King told the youth of how he was a brigand in the mountains, and of his manner of life there, and how he was captured and brought to Ispahan. But yet the youth told not the King of how *he* had come into captivity. And when it was quite dark the King said "Behold oh youth, this is not the first time that I have been in this prison. Once before I was in it, and I escaped from it. Let us now therefore see whether the same may not be done again. And, if it may, then, as thou art a youth of goodly disposition, I will take thee with me, and lead thee to the mountains, and thou shalt become a brigand even as I." And the King went to one of the windows of the prison, and lo! a bar was loose; and he took it out, so that there was room for a man's body to pass out through the window. And the King climbed out, and the youth followed him. And the King jumped down to the grounds, and the youth jumped too.

Now, in order that he might pass through the window, the King had taken off his cloak, and was naked, save for his loin-cloth. And he was a man of goodly proportions, noble to look upon, with a mighty body, and long limbs. And as he stood naked, save for his loin-cloth, the moonlight shone upon him. And the youth looked upon him, and thought in his heart "By Allah! What is the village blacksmith compared with this man?" And a desire to be close to the King entered into the mind of the youth, and he said "Oh my friend, let me lean upon thy arm, for in jumping from the window I have hurt my foot, and it pains me to walk on it." And before the King could answer, the youth leant upon his arm, and so they walked together. And in a little while the King said "It is too late tonight to go to the mountains. I know of a house in the city where we may tarry for the night; it is the house of a friend, and he has given me the key." And the youth said "It is well"; and a desire to be yet closer to the King entered into his mind, and he said "Is the house far off? For truly my foot grows worse, and it is a grievous pain to me when it touches the ground; therefore, oh my friend, if the house be not far off, take me up into thine arms, and carry me thither." And the King said "Thou art a well-grown youth, and assuredly no light burden; yet, since the house is not far off, I will carry thee thither." And he took the youth up into his arms, and after a little the youth lay his hand, as it were by accident, upon the King's hand, and pressed it. But the King paid no heed; and when they came to a certain house, he set down the youth, and unlocked the door, and they went in. And there was a room, with a lamp burning, and food and wine set forth, and two couches, one at one end of the room and one at the other. And when they had eaten and drunk and conversed for a little space, the King said "Now it is meet that we should sleep; for the hour is late, and we must rise up early in the morning. Therefore sleep thou upon that couch, and I will sleep upon this." And the youth blushed and said "Oh my friend, before we sleep, grant me, I beseech thee, one favour. For thou hast brought me out of captivity, and saved me from death and torments, and hast been unto me even as a benefactor or a father; and so, I pray thee, let me, in token of my gratitude, kiss thee upon the lips." And the King replied "I thank thee, youth, I thank thee. Yet am I not one that is given overmuch to kissing. Therefore go thou and sleep upon thy couch, while I sleep upon mine." And he turned away, and went to his couch, and took off his cloak and his loin-cloth, and then wrapped himself again in his cloak, and lay down. And the youth, looking, saw the private parts of the King, and his whole body naked; and all the madness of love rushed into his soul.

And he lay down upon his couch, trembling and distracted, thinking of the beauty and the strength of the King's body; and he thought "Truly this man is a great man and a noble man, though he be but a brigand, and he is worthy of my love." And a furious desire burnt within him to lie with the King. And, when he could master the desire no longer, he rose up, and went to the King's couch, and knelt beside it. And he said "Oh my friend, art thou awake?" And the King said "I am awake; what wouldst

thou?" And the youth said "One thing only, oh my benefactor.
Let me, I beg thee, show my gratitude towards thee, or I shall sleep
not, all the night through. For is it fitting that such great benefits
as thou hast shown unto me should pass unrequited? Therefore,
oh my friend, let me embrace thee once. But haply thou thinkest
that I ask for this thing out of lasciviousness. But by Allah it is
not so. By Allah, it is not out of lasciviousness that I would
embrace thee, but as a token of friendship and the gratitude that
is in my heart." And the King answered "I thank thee youth, I
thank thee. Yet am I not one that is given overmuch to embracing.
Therefore go thou and sleep upon thy couch, and I will sleep upon
mine." And the youth rose up in silence, and went back to his couch,
and lay once more upon it. And he was filled with shame and
despair. And he thought "What is this that I have done? And how
have I disgraced myself! Oh, truly, I am a miserable youth, for I
have professed myself to this unknown man, this brigand, and
he has despised me and turned me away, and will have none of
me, and yet his scorn has not quenched my desire. Rather it has
increased it. And now he loathes me in his heart as a lascivious
shameless youth; and I have sworn falsely and taken the name of
Allah in vain." And he groaned inwardly. And then he thought
"But perchance it is not so; perchance he believed what I said;
perchance he does not loathe me; perchance he loves me; and
perchance he was cold towards me because of my coldness towards him. If I had wooed him boldly and without disguise, then
might he not –?" And the tears rose to the youth's eyes, and he
pressed his hands against his head in anguish. And he thought "O
unhappy that I am! For if this be indeed so, how can I discover
it? How can I go back once more to his couch, and proffer myself
again? For if he loves me not, then how despitefully will he use
me, and what a vile wretch will he think me! And why should I
dream that he loves me? What sign has he shown?" And then he
tried to sleep, but could not, and tossed backwards and forwards
on the couch. And he thought "Would I were back again in
prison! For surely I would rather be beaten with rods, and nailed
hand and foot to the pillory in the market-place, and have my
head cut off, and my body thrown to the dogs, than suffer what I
suffer now." And then all at once anger and pride came into his
heart, and he thought "Who is this man that he should treat me
thus? Do I deserve such scorn? Am I indeed so uncomely a thing

to look upon? What? Has not the King himself looked upon me with love, and shall this man, this brigand, dare to be indifferent towards me?" And like one mad and half drunk, he rose suddenly from his couch, and, casting his cloak from him, went naked to the King's. And he knelt beside it, and said "Oh my friend, sleepest thou?" And the King answered, as one waking from sleep, "What wouldst thou? I was dreaming of the valleys of Cashmere." And the youth said "I love thee; I desire thee; let me lie with thee this night." And the King replied "I thank thee, youth, I thank thee. But truly I would rather dream of the valleys of Cashmere." Then the youth rose up in anger and said "Why dost thou treat me thus? Do I deserve such scorn? Am I indeed so uncomely a thing to look upon? Is it a small thing that I should proffer myself to thee? Know that the – know that a certain great one has looked upon me with love; and who art thou to use me despitefully? A brigand from the mountains. And I offer thee favours, and thou wilt none of them; and I give thee my body, and thou turnest away; and my love, and thou talkest of the valleys of Cashmere." And then the King said. "Youth, lie down beside me on the couch, and I will tell thee a story."

So the youth lay down beside the King, and the King said – "There was once a King who loved a shepherd youth, and sent him many presents. But the youth cared not for the King, and used him unkindly, and the King –" but when the King had spoken so far, the youth shivered, and cried out in a loud voice. "Who art thou?" for he had suddenly guessed that it was the King. And the King said "I am a certain great one – among the brigands." And the youth said "My lord, is it the King?" But the King laid his hand on the youth's shoulder and said "What matters it who I am? Wilt thou not let me finish my story?" And the youth said "my friend speaks truly. Yet methinks I have guessed the story, for does it not end with the youth repenting of his unkindness to the King? – Does it not end so?" And the King said "Does it end so? Nay, I know not." And the youth said "Oh my friend, tell me this; if the youth repented of his unkindness to the King, would the brigand repent of his unkindness to – to his servant?" And the King pressed the shoulder of the youth, and answered "Oh youth, thou hast performed a miracle; for I verily believe that thou hast cured my wounds. Stretch forth thy hand therefore, and untie my bandages, and feel whether I be not whole."

And neither the King nor the youth slept that night. But at the second hour after the dawn they rose up and departed.

And at the third hour after the dawn, the King's chamberlain pulled aside the curtains of his bedchamber, and admitted the Captains and the Counsellors. And the King lay in his bed of state. And beside him stood the youth, dressed in fine raiment of silk and gold, with a silken turban on his head, and golden ornaments on his arms, and precious pearls in his ears. And the King said to those assembled "Behold my servant, whom it is my delight to honour. Oh my servant, what are thy wishes, that they may be granted?" And the youth bowed low, and said "My lord has granted all my wishes; yet have I one wish that I beg my lord may grant likewise." And the King said "Speak, what is it?" And the youth bent down and whispered in the King's ear "It is that I may lie tonight with a certain great one among the brigands." And the King said aloud "Thou shalt have thy wish."

But when the blacksmith and the Princess Fatima learnt all that had passed, they –

– But with these words, the beauteous and discreet Scheherezade, seeing through the window the first rays of the morning light, tactfully paused . . .

COMMENTARY
"THE HASCHISH"

This poem was written between September 1906 and December 1908. Lytton Strachey wrote a good deal of poetry, almost all of it in a romantic vein of which this may be taken as typical. There is no biographical evidence that Strachey ever took hashish, but the concordance of the experience related in this poem to contemporary descriptions of experiences with hallucinogenic drugs suggests that if he did not then someone must have given him a particularly graphic and accurate account of the effects of the drug. The delight in ambiguity, the pleasure in discovering a contradiction and passively witnessing its mystical resolution, the aphrodisiacal heightening of sexual fantasies and experiences, the visions, and the feeling that each of one's senses is doing the job of one of the others, are all phenomena reported by users of cannabis resin. The use of this drug was not so common in Strachey's day as it is at present, but there were then no penalties. It is obvious not only from the positive attitude manifested towards the drug in this poem, but also from his general social views, that were Lytton Strachey alive today his voice would be added to the chorus of voices deploring the existing laws on soft drugs.

"The Haschish" is a very good specimen of the drug-inspired poem. It lacks the vigour of Coleridge's "Kubla Khan", whose line is shorter by one foot; its obvious affinities are with the more languorous productions of Poe and Baudelaire; and perhaps its imagery owes something to Swinburne. But it is not an entirely derivative effort, and the reader may think it compares favourably with some of today's equally romantic but less disciplined attempts at expressing much the same thing.

"The Haschish" originally appeared in the *New Statesman and Nation* Literary Supplement for 26 June 1937.

THE HASCHISH

Oh, let me dream, and let me know no more
The sun's harsh sight and life's discordant roar;
Let me eclipse my being in a swoon,
And, lingering through a long penumbral noon,
Feel like a ghost a soft Elysian balm,
A universe of amaranthine calm,
Devoid of thought, forgetful of desire,
And quiet as joined hearts where still suspire
Love's ultimate tendernesses, while faint bliss
With pale mandragora drowns the accomplished kiss!
So shall I find, inextricably sweet,
The phantom realm where all vagaries meet,
Where strangest visions unreluctant rise,
And wonder's self's oblivious of surprise.
There lost among impossibles I'll rest,
Ambiguousness shall lull me on her breast,
And heavenliest contradictions soothe my sense
And fold my soul in soft inconsequence.
Confused I'll vaguely taste and strangely hear,
Feel with the eye, and whisper with the ear,
And half-experience and half-surmise,
Imagine, and remember, and improvise,
And laugh with melancholy, and just weep,
And dwindle through infinitudes of sleep.
Ah! Ah! To swoon away beyond the touch
Of this wrong world's too little or too much,
To melt ineffably, and gradually find

The really interesting question

Far more enchantments for the fading mind
Than poets ever wot of – Starry showers
Of magical smells distilled from unknown flowers,
Blushes of angels, immanence of eyes,
Smiles from the moon, faint jewels, fairy sighs,
Aerial oceans, and liquid halls
And Virgil murmuring from the virginals!
Oh Soft! Oh delicate, and sweetly wound
Into one substance with the calm profound
Of visionary being! All my thought,
As heavy incense wanders into nought,
In hanging dissipation drifts and dies
Through subtle and through mystic harmonies,
Where vague remembrance finds delicious fare –
Looks that are felt, and lusts as light as air,
And curious embraces like September flowers
Vanishing down interminable hours,
And love's last kiss, exquisitely withdrawn,
And copulations dimmer than the dawn.
Who now shall fret? Who now shall strive and smart,
When swimming ease buoys up the unloaded heart,
When the freed soul explores unending rest,
And wrapped in wonders, infinitely blest,
Divines through worlds of glory vanishing wings,
And moves ecstatic towards immortal things –
Embodied sounds more pure than e'er could flow
From Palestrina joined with Angelo?
This is the happy end, the promised peace!
Divine Giorgione glows o'er more than Greece,
And in warm shadows nectared fountains fall,
And changing music trembles over all –
Enormous music swooning over shores
Drowned in Autumnal grandeur, till the doors
Of remote heaven swing round on oilèd hinge
Enchanted, and the faint evasive fringe
Of all occult and unimagined joys
Waves into vision – forms of golden boys
Embraced seraphically in far lands
By languid lover, linking marvellous hands
With early virgins crowned with quiet wreaths

168

The haschish

Of lily, frailer than the air that breathes
The memory of Sappho all day long
Through Lesbian shades of fragmentary song,
Immortal, holy, dim, dim, holy, lost
Infinitely in dreams emmeshed and crossed
By fluctuating nothings, where the deep
Strange soul dissolved in alabaster sleep
Melts slowly and beautifully, even as mine own,
Half echoing and forgetting loves long known
And long forbidden, fades through dreamy streams
Dreaming, and dreaming dreams of dreamier dreams
– Dreams that mysteriously themselves enlace
With Archipiada's – Archipiada's – face.

AFTERWORD

Few readers can fail to notice the relevance of many of these pieces to contemporary social concerns. Where the intention of the piece is propagandistic or persuasive, it may serve some commendable purpose to make Strachey's feelings and views known to a broader public than they originally reached. But the collection as a whole shows that Strachey, in his private life, devoted a good deal of his time and not a little of his skill as a writer to the consideration of social issues; and, by extension, that his audiences in Cambridge and Bloomsbury are not quite so open to the charge of callousness or lack of concern about social questions.

Most of the pieces included here were written when Strachey was in his twenties and thirties: the very topics he chose to write about are indicative of his radicalism, and are the same ones that engage the youth of today. War and conscription and sexual roles and practices may not be questions of perennial concern to youth, but they become of paramount importance in certain historical conditions: for example, when a large body of opinion holds that an unjust war is being waged; and when young people become totally disaffected, perhaps as a result of war or injustice, with the life-styles and attitudes of their parents.

There are obvious parallels to be drawn between the circumstances of a young man born in 1880, whose political consciousness dawned with the Boer War, who came to maturity in the Edwardian era, and who had the promise of a more civilized existence broken by the First World War; and the circumstances of today's youth, whose visions of civilization were nurtured in the early sixties only to be disabused by the cold war and Vietnam. These circumstances themselves make for radicalism.

But the radicalism of people born into affluence, like Strachey, and like many of today's activist youth, is very different from the radicalism that springs from poverty; it is not the political radicalism even of the middle-class individual who sees his own and his civilization's salvation as necessarily allied with the working-class movement. It is a bourgeois radicalism, as befits the middle-class origins of its proponents. It is a *personal* radicalism, and its focus is on individuals and not movements; it may be caused by the perception of the evils of war and injustice, but the reason for it is most often disaffection with the ways of the older generation. It rejects reform and a mere tinkering with the parts of a whole that is fundamentally corrupt and degenerate, and it rejects not just some aspects of the older generation's manners and values, but their entire life-style.

This personal radicalism is not of necessity incompatible with political radicalism, it simply has its origins in different circumstances. The goals are the same, to live a decent life in a world that is free of war and injustice, and both often reject the same aspects of their society; but sometimes the means by which they seek to achieve the new society are so different as to engender hostility between them. Strachey and the new personal radicals can appear to be unconcerned about their own privilege, and to be indifferent to the quality of life as it is lived by people beneath them on the social ladder, who may appear to come to their attention only when they are victims of an injustice so blatant as to attract publicity. For their part the new radicals tended to regard the parties and movements of the political radicals as being part of the existing system, and as corrupt and fundamentally unsound as the parties of the majority.

One striking difference between Strachey's era and our own is that very few of the intellectuals of his day would have regarded the issues touched upon in this collection as being social issues at all. They would have felt most of these problems to be ethical ones, and cases for individual deliberation and private resolution. To us it seems almost obvious that Strachey was dealing with social problems – and so it seemed to him. If there is an element of prophecy in Strachey's attitude to these questions, it is not in the answers he suggests to them, but in the congruence of his point of view to our own.

P.L. 1972.

INDEX

Observer, 10
Oedipus Rex, 85
Olivier, Lord, 17n
Olivier, the Hon. Noel, 17n, 18, 24, 32, 34
overpopulation, 107, 108–10

Parmoor, Lord, 18n, 20, 25
Plato: dialogues as source for "Diary of an Athenian", 135; *Phaedrus*, 130, 135; *The Republic*, 135; *The Symposium*, 135
pleasure, as principle of life, 66
Poe, Edgar Allen, 166
Pollock, Sir Frederick, 121, 127
"pro-Germanism" in Bloomsbury, 5, 18n, 19

Queen Victoria, 85

Rabelais, 85, 87
Ramsey, Frank, xii
Recruiting and Exemption Tribunals, 8, 12, 14, 15, 19, 27, 29, 30; Lytton Strachey's appearance before Hampstead, 21n, 22, 23
Redford, George Alexander, 71, 74
Reid, Robert Threshie, *see* Loreburn, Earl
Renan, Ernest, 86
Repington, Charles à Court, Colonel, 12n, 14, 16, 19, 20
repression of emotions among English, 124–5
Rimbaud, 33, 34
Robertson, William (Sir), 9n, 10–11
Rothiemurchus, the Grants of ("the Family"), 35n, 37
Russell, Bertrand, xi, xiv, 5, 6n, 17, 26, 28, 29, 32, 34, 122; *Principles of Social Reconstruction*, 35n, 39; prosecution of, 34n, 35

Sanger, C. P., xi, 12n, 14, 17
Sargant-Florence, Alix (Mrs James Strachey), 35n, 37
Scott, C. P. ("Pa"), 17n, 17, 20, 24

Sennacherib: historical account of, 40; fictional dialogue with Rupert Brooke, 42–4
Shakespeare, William, 68, 85; *Othello*, 84; *Romeo and Juliet*, 80, 130
Shaw, George Bernard, 71
Shove, Gerald, xii, 7n, 8, 39
Shove, Mrs Gerald *see* Maitland, Fredegond
Sidgwick, Henry, 101, 103
Simon, Sir John, 5, 13, 20
Snowden, Philip (Viscount Snowden), 28n, 29, 31n, 32, 24
Spectator, 39, 71; James Strachey sacked from, 4, 9, 12, 21n; *see also* Strachey, John St Loe
Stephen, Adrian, 12–13n, 15, 16n
Stephen, Karin, 13n, 16n
Stephen, Sir Leslie, 12n
Stephen, Vanessa, *see* Bell, Vanessa
Stephen, Virginia, *see* Woolf, Virginia
Sterne, Laurence, 85; *Tristram Shandy*, 90
Strachey, Dorothy, 31n
Strachey, James, x, xii–xiv, 4–5, 6–39 *passim*, 40; application for conscientious objector status, 11; definition of conscientious objection, 19; statement to Recruitment and Exemption Tribunal, 8; *see also Spectator*, and *Manchester Guardian*
Strachey, (Joan) Pernel, 11n, 12, 34
Strachey, John St Loe, 4, 21n, 23, 71, 73
Strachey, Lytton: attitude to censorship, xiii; attitude to conscription, xiii, 3; dissertation on Warren Hastings, 101; *Eminent Victorians*, ix, 3, 35n; *Landmarks in French Literature*, ix, 62; leaflet for National Council against Conscription, 4–5; *Lord Pettigrew*, political topics to be included, 45; "Militarism and Theology", 3;

Index